How To...

PLAY OUTSIDE GUITAR LICKS

Mastering the Symmetrical Diminished Scale

By Chris Buono

T0079156

To access video visit:
www.halleonard.com/mylibrary

Enter Code
3180-5343-7597-1149

Cover Photo by Will Eagan

ISBN 978-1-4950-0814-6

HAL•LEONARD®

7777 W. BLUEMOUND RD. P.O. BOX 13819 MILWAUKEE, WI 53213

In Australia Contact:
Hal Leonard Australia Pty. Ltd.
4 Lentara Court
Cheltenham, Victoria, 3192 Australia
Email: ausadmin@halleonard.com.au

Visit Hal Leonard Online at
www.halleonard.com

CONTENTS

Page

3   Foreword
4   About the Author
4   Dedication
4   Acknowledgments
5   Testimonials
5   Introduction
6   The Approach
6   About the Video

7   **CHAPTER 1: Symmetrical Diminished 101**
7   Introducing the Symmetrical Diminished Scale
10   Formula
12   The Symmetrical Factor
13   Chord Applications

14   **CHAPTER 2: Vertical Fingerings**
14   Vertical Positional
17   Zig-Zag Positional
20   Zig-Zag/Vertical Hybrid Positional
20   Full Neck Vision

23   **CHAPTER 3: Nested Symmetrical Components**
23   Nested Symmetrical Intervals
28   Nested Diminished Seventh Arpeggios

33   **CHAPTER 4: Line Construction and Application**
33   Static Improvisation
39   Playing Over Changes

49   **CHAPTER 5: Harmonic Connections**
49   Tetrad Foundations

56   **CHAPTER 6: Symmetrical Diminished Pentatonic Scales**
57   SDP 1–#9–#4–5–♭7
59   SDP 1–#9–3–#4–6
61   SDP 1–♭9–3–#4–6
63   SDP 1–♭9–3–#4–♭7

FOREWORD

In the summer of 1994, I was performing at Wetlands Preserve in the Tribeca section of New York City. To anyone who regularly performed there, and everyone who frequented the club, it was just "Wetlands"—a legendary room right outside the Holland Tunnel known for great sound and passionate music fans. On a good night, it wasn't uncommon to see a line out the door extending down Hudson Street. It was one of these nights during a Screaming Headless Torsos gig to a packed house that I noticed a scrappy-looking college kid in the front row.

By this time, I could tell who the musicians were in the crowd, and this guy clearly had "guitar player" written all over his face. Not once did he move from his spot, nor did he seem to lose an ounce of focus from the music (not to mention my hands). He was intensely taking it all in. It was as if you could see the wheels spinning in his head.

As I was packing up my gear after the gig, I noticed him walking up the steps to the stage. I met him at the top step, prepared for whatever exchange was about to take place, when, before I could say a word, he politely said, "Hey, my name is Chris. Do you give lessons?" That's how I met Chris Buono, and I've watched his focused wheels spin ever since.

More than 20 years later, Chris is still the perpetually inquisitive guitar player who came to my door on 10th Street in the East Village soon after that Wetlands gig. The focus I saw that night was real. He brought it to everything he took on—not only as a player, sideman, bandleader, writer, educator, and definitely as an author, but also as a person, a husband, a father, and my friend.

Chris has written a thoughtful and in-depth book on a very underused and, at the same time, overused scale: symmetrical diminished. You could say it's a meditation! This octatonic scale is an infamously tough animal to wrap your mind and ears around, let alone your fingers. Producing an odd sound that can be mysterious and unresolved that keeps repeating itself every minor 3rd, it's a daunting yet beautiful animal to tame.

The unique symmetrical nature of this scale is almost always misused as a mere cookie-cutter line generator. The status quo is to simply show you a lick and subsequently repeat it in three other places on the neck. Sadly, the result is often predictable and consequently boring. Chris breaks symmetrical diminished down and explains in detail what it *really* is and how to *really* visualize it on the guitar. Chris' approach will teach you how to make creative choices with the symmetrical diminished scale as opposed to just meandering through a pattern of repeating shapes.

Improvising at any level takes not only focus, but also unrelenting commitment. I believe Chris applied every bit of his focus and fully committed himself to giving anyone who reads this book a thorough, well-thought perspective on playing outside lines with the symmetrical diminished scale. If this is your goal, you've focused on the right book.

David Fiuczynski

Screaming Headless Torsos
Professor | Berklee College of Music

ABOUT THE AUTHOR

Photo by John Buono

Heralded as a "multi-media guitar madman," Chris Buono infiltrates the modern guitar world from myriad directions. Be it in audio, in video, in book form, or in the minds of gear aficionados, his reach is vast. At the forefront is Buono's passion for conveying knowledge to those who are willing to work for it. Through 20+ years of teaching in just about every forum a guitarist can—including five years as a professor in the esteemed Guitar Department at Berklee College of Music and currently as a prolific TrueFire artist and video clinician for Guitarinstructor.com—Chris Buono has helped propel students from all over the world to new heights.

For everything and more about Chris Buono, go to:

- http://www.chrisbuono.com/
- http://www.facebook.com/pages/Chris-Buono/179100172190?ref=hl
- https://twitter.com/ChrisBuono
- http://www.youtube.com/user/chrisbuonovideos?feature=mhum
- https://soundcloud.com/chrisbuonotracks
- https://www.instagram.com/chrisbuono/

DEDICATION

This book is dedicated to one of the nicest human beings I've ever known. At every turn, John Clarizio was there. You are missed, my friend.

ACKNOWLEDGMENTS

Anything and everything I do starts with my family: my amazing wife and best friend, Stacy, whom I love beyond words, and our two boys, John & Wil, who make us so very proud and keep our lives an adventure each and every day. Thanks to Jeff Schroedl for giving me an opportunity to get these crazy ideas on paper and always displaying saintly patience. A long overdue thanks goes to Jeff Peretz for introducing me to the world of playing outside in a single life-changing lesson I took from him in 1990. Forever thanks to Dave Fiuczynski and Wayne Krantz for their guidance and inspiration, with an extra nod to Wayne for turning me on to the symmetrical diminished scale. Life-long gratitude goes to Gerry Carboy, Vic Juris, and Frankie Cicala for setting me on this path, both in improvising and in teaching. The most special thank you to Brad Wendkos for relentless support and encouragement, and never letting me forget how good life is. A brotherly shout out goes to Steve Jenkins, Vernon Reid, Oz Noy, and Bob Lanzetti for always being there to lend an ear and to share some laughs. The biggest and best high five to Kieran Downes of Downes Guitars for including me in his guitar building journey and for outfitting this project with the coolest orange guitar ever made. Finally, a heartfelt thanks to all my students who have worked through these concepts with me—most notably Dan Christian and George Vanderbilt.

"Chris Buono is insane. If you're reading this book, it's already too late—you're in his world now. The reality of that situation is this: you're only a half or whole step away from nirvana, and this book will show you how you to get there."
–Vernon Reid

"Chris Buono delivers a book that will give even the most experienced players a whole new set of tools for making their playing sound fresh, bold, and *out*!"
–Oz Noy

"An extremely well organized and thorough book on the symmetrical diminished scale, Chris seems to preemptively answer many of the questions one may have. In-depth explanation of the theory behind the scale, when and why to use it, and tons of musical examples make this book a great tool for any player looking to get more color in their improvisations."
–Bob Lanzetti

"I highly recommend this book for guitarists of all stylistic stripes, but especially those who are looking to learn more about outside sounds and tones that can add just the right amount of 'quirk' needed for unique, modern phrasing. The examples and diagrams Chris has put together are clear, inspiring road maps that will quickly enable players to come up with their own melodic and harmonic ideas."
–Mark Lettieri

"Legendary guitarists such as Pat Martino and Robben Ford have long preached the power of the symmetrical diminished scale. Sadly, a majority of guitarists have no real idea how to harness the magic of this simple eight-note pattern. Don't be in that majority. Learn what's in this great book from Chris Buono and you won't be."
–Jude Gold

"Chris has come up with one of the best books I've ever seen for mastering this most tricky of scales. The diminished scale is notoriously hard to get down for guitar players, but Chris has developed a multitude of fantastic and easy-to-follow ideas for learning the scale, developing vocabulary, and applying it that make this journey so much more approachable and musical. If you ever felt intimidated by the diminished scale, you *need* this book!"
–Tom Quayle

INTRODUCTION

Not too long after I started playing the guitar, I discovered two lifelong loves that have stayed with me throughout my career: pedals and improvisation. The former is a subject all its own and for another time, but it should come as no surprise the latter set me on a path that led to this book. A big part of my improvisational endeavors are rooted in pushing the boundaries of both harmony and melody. The push is often propelled by my unavoidable intentions of taking what I am playing over somewhere outside of where it is. There's that word, "outside." Let's talk about it.

What is "outside?" To me, it's playing outside the confines of what most people judge as tonal, safe-sounding, and/or continuously-pleasing-to-the-ear musical instances. Of course, what's "inside" is a totally objective call. That all said, it's safe to assume more often than not that most of us with an ear will agree when inside is no longer in, and the music has entered the outside realm. What this really comes down to is not what playing outside is; rather, it's *why* we play outside. While this is not the forum for what could be a doctorate-level introspection into the human mind's musical preferences, I'll go out on a limb and throw this out there: I play outside because it's awesome.

In *How to Play Outside Guitar Licks*, you'll take a good, deep look at the outside concept with the incredible octatonic scale. Through an exhaustive probe into this single scale, you'll come away with a newfound vision for what symmetrical diminished is, what it can do, and what more you can do with it. This book is the product of thousands of hours of trial and error. I wish nothing more than for you to take this information and make music that inspires you!

THE APPROACH

The title of the book has the word "play" in it, and that's exactly what you'll be doing—a *lot*. With every concept, there will be loads of playing examples supported by detailed explanations so you can not only play what's in front of you, but also learn how to play your own outside licks with the symmetrical diminished scale. Even better, the video content that accompanies this book contains demonstrations of each and every line (and exercise) played by me.

With any intense scale study at this level comes a horde of fingerings. Contained within this book is a large cache of symmetrical diminished fingerings as well as in-depth probes into what's under the hood of those fingerings. To support those fingerings are finger patterns and scale degree layouts, as well as naming conventions to best organize that which could quickly make your guitar neck snow blind!

Speaking of fingerings, a common first impression of symmetrical diminished scales is by way of horizontal-based fingerings. However, this book takes a different path by introducing you to vertically positioned scale fingerings that are organized into what I call "Fingering Groups." What's more, there will be emphasis put on nested intervals and arpeggios, connections to chord shapes, and even alternate approaches to scale formula. Every effort was made to help guide you to this book's end goal: fully visualizing and ultimately mastering the symmetrical diminished scale so you can consistently play great outside guitar lines!

Special note: Given the nature of the symmetrical diminished scale and the enharmonic possibilities it breeds, the standard notation part of every musical example was approached with the following considerations:

1. There are enharmonic possibilities that result from strictly following the symmetrical diminished formula that are not common to everyday theory speak (not to mention what someone who reads music prefers to see on a chart). Adjustments were made where needed, such as avoiding accidentals applied to the natural half steps (E♯/F♭ or B♯/C♭) as a result of the formula. However, if an example was rooted in a key where a note is diatonically one of those designations—such as the 3rd of C♯ being E♯—then that's what is written.

2. There are no double sharps or double flats written in the notation part of the examples. In explanations pertaining to fully diminished seventh chord formulas and arpeggios, it's required to note the correct procedure in which that chord is derived, which includes a ♭♭7. Keep that in mind when encountering this element.

ABOUT THE VIDEO

You'll find performances of all the examples—both lines and exercises—on the accompanying online video included with this book. Follow the instructions on page 1 to access all the videos. The example numbers will correspond with the file names, however, if the example is a line, there will be the word "SLOW" or "FAST" appended to the file name. "SLOW" indicates lines played at a slow to medium tempo, while "FAST" indicates a faster tempo. The specific tempo of each example is also included in the video filenames.

CHAPTER 1

SYMMETRICAL DIMINISHED 101

To play outside lines with the symmetrical diminished scale, it's a good idea to first learn about the basic mechanics, formula, and inherent symmetrical properties of the scale. That is, after a proper introduction.

INTRODUCING THE SYMMETRICAL DIMINISHED SCALE

Below is a symmetrical diminished scale in what I call a ZZVHP #1, or Zig-Zag/Vertical Hybrid Positional #1 form, presented in the key of C.

C Symmetrical Diminished Scale

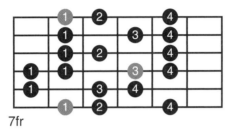

Your first order of business is to play the above fingering, which is the first of many you'll learn in this book. Play it up and down the neck in all 12 keys. While you're at it, be sure to focus on the root. Once you have a handle on the fingering, have some fun playing these 12 lines (one for each key) to get an idea of the symmetrical diminished scale in action.

▶ Example 1

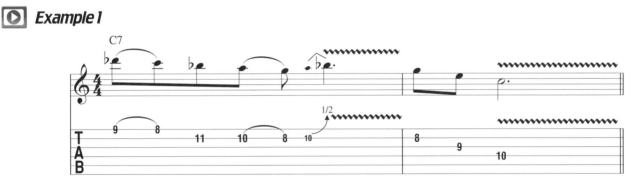

▶ Example 2

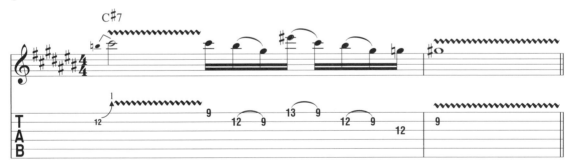

▶ Example 3

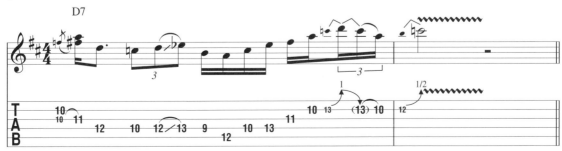

Example 4

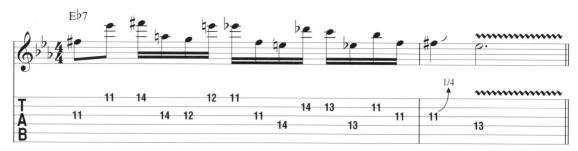

Example 5

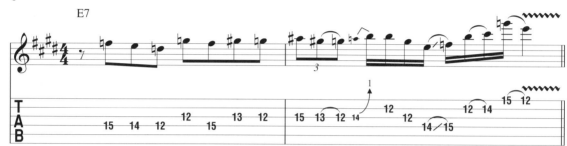

Example 6

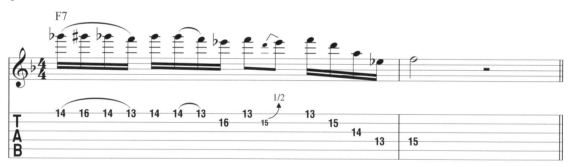

Example 7

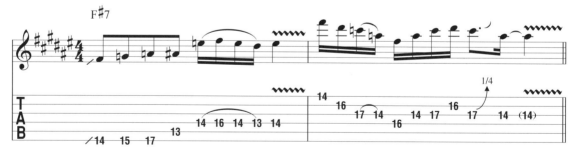

Example 8

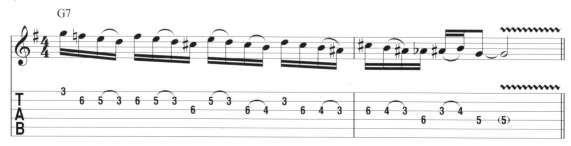

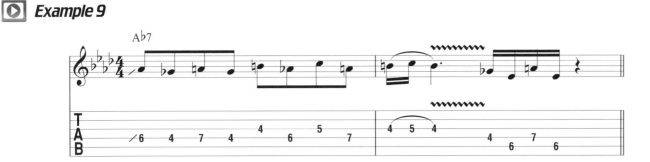

Example 9

Example 10

Example 11

Example 12

While you're playing through these 12 outside-sounding symmetrical diminished-based lines and getting introduced to what this scale can do, let's start looking at its foundational components, as well as what's to come.

The Basic Facts

Some basic facts about the symmetrical diminished scale you'll learn in more depth throughout the book are:

- It has eight notes.
- It has more than one name.
- It has signature adjacent string fingering patterns.
- There are several repeating, cyclical (symmetrical) elements nested in the scale.
- The primary application is playing over various types of dominant chords.

Steps

Pioneering music theorist George Russell defined a scale as "a fundamental order of elements." Applying this definition to conventional scales, including the diatonic major and melodic minor scales as well as their modes, the basic elements are whole and half steps. The order of a scale's steps is what shapes its sound and character. It is with those attributes we assess their function and application. The symmetrical diminished scale is a simple order of elements that consists of repeating half step/whole step sequences. This cycle of alternating half steps and whole steps happens four times per octave, resulting in an eight-note-per-octave scale—one note larger than the common seven-note or *heptatonic* scales you likely work with on a daily basis. This eight-note configuration makes the symmetrical diminished scale *octatonic*.

Names

The symmetrical diminished scale has a few alternative names such as:

- Half step/whole step scale

- Half whole diminished

- Dominant diminished

- Double diminished

As we learn more about the symmetrical diminished scale and how to play lines with it while exploring the concepts throughout the rest of the book, these alternative names will be justified. In regards to the first name—half step/whole step scale—that describes the scale's step order already discussed.

Another name sometimes used to identify this octatonic melodic device is "diminished scale." While there are logical reasons as to why that name could be considered a valid choice, it's prone to confusion. This stems from a simple notion: if you can have a scale built on a cycle of half steps and whole steps, then what about one built on a whole/half cycle? It is how we interpret the scale formula by way of scale degree numbers that will clear up this conundrum.

FORMULA

Steps notwithstanding, the way to definitively define a scale's function is the scale degree numbering system. When it comes to most heptatonic scales, a formula consisting of integers from 1 to 7 will suffice. For instance, the major scale is as follows:

$$1 \quad 2 \quad 3 \quad 4 \quad 5 \quad 6 \quad 7$$

Scale formula is conveyed in various combinations of raised (sharped) and lowered (flatted) degrees as compared to the basic major scale formula seen above. This is called *parallel major comparison* and is effective in conveying the individual components of any and all scales. Some examples are:

- **Lydian:**   1 2 3 ♯4 5 6 7
- **Melodic Minor:**   1 2 ♭3 4 5 6 7
- **Lydian Dominant:**   1 2 3 ♯4 5 6 ♭7
- **Harmonic Minor:**   1 2 ♭3 4 5 ♭6 7
- **Phrygian Major:**   1 ♭2 3 4 5 ♭6 ♭7
- **Harmonic Major:**   1 2 3 4 5 ♭6 7
- **Lydian Diminished:** 1 2 ♭3 ♯4 5 6 7

The major scale formula is also what is used to convey additions and subtractions to the conventional heptatonic formula. For example, the ever-present pentatonic scale in its various forms consists of five notes. Those five-note formulas are based off a subtracted seven-note heptatonic major scale formula. When it comes to adding notes to the basic seven-note formula, such as the case with octatonic scales, one of the degrees must be doubled while not repeating itself—e.g., ♭5 and ♯5. That all said, the symmetrical diminished scale is not only an octatonic scale that requires an addition to the heptatonic formula, but it's also part of a small group of scales whose formula, while still rooted in parallel major comparison, requires a more involved scale degree designation system.

In its most basic state, the symmetrical diminished scale formula is:

1	♭2	♯2	3	♯4	5	6	♭7

As expected, there is a doubled degree: the 2nd degree. While this is an accurate listing of the symmetrical diminished scale formula, there's more to it than that. The following is a more involved, yet applicable formula:

1	♭9	♯9/♭3	3	♯4/♭5/♯11	5	6/13	♭7

Let's break down what's contained in this version by reviewing, and at times, expanding on what you've learned so far.

- The symmetrical diminished scale is primarily used for playing over various types of dominant seventh chords, as well as substitute diminished seventh chords acting as dominant chords. What connects symmetrical diminished to dominant chords are the 3rd and ♭7th degrees, seen in both versions of the formula listed. Tetrad-based harmony is centered on 3's and 7's. The heart of any dominant seventh chord type is the tension between its 3rd and ♭7th chord tones, also known as a tritone (see note below). To add, this notion justifies one half of one of the other alternative names—dominant diminished—with the first term referring to that use.

- To justify the dominant chord-based focus of symmetrical diminished, take away the altered degrees as well as the 6th degree, and you're left with a basic dominant seventh chord formula. This strengthens its case as a powerful option for when you find yourself blowing over stock drop 2 and drop 3 dominant seventh chord voicings.

- Given the symmetrical diminished scale's relationship to dominant seventh chords, it makes more sense to consistently consider the two altered 2nd degrees as altered 9ths. This thinking also applies to the ♯4th and 6th degrees being sometimes seen as ♯11th and 13th, respectively.

- To understand the logic behind the diminished seventh-for-dominant seventh substitution concept, take away the ♯9, ♯11, and 13 degrees and then swap the root for the ♭9. This leaves you with a diminished seventh arpeggio chord formula strengthening the case for the construction of edgy, yet invigorating lines over dominant seventh chords by way of symmetrical diminished.

- Notice that ♯9 is also identified as "♭3" in the above formula. While there will be much attention paid to this part of the scale in reference to the altered 9's, there are very cool substitution ideas with regards to the ♯9's enharmonic relationship to ♭3. When considering that degree as a ♭3, it sparks minor blues and partial major blues ideas, not to mention superimposed diatonic minor, minor 6th, and minor 7th arpeggios, among others.

- Take note of the triple naming of the fourth note in the formula: ♯4/♭5/♯11. First, the ♯4 and ♭5 elements are enharmonically related. The ♯11 denotes the same note up an octave and subsequent octaves. When naming chords with these alterations/tensions, it's common for guitarists to freely use them interchangeably. It's for that reason the formula represents them all.

Understanding basic symmetrical diminished principles such as these makes understanding outside lines that much easier. With that in mind, be aware that throughout the book, true to guitar player form, I'll interchange scale degree designations where needed with supporting explanations.

Tri-what?
Throughout this book, as well as any study on outside playing and/or advanced improvisation, you'll run into the term *tritone*, which means three (tri-) whole steps (-tone). From a root, three whole steps away can be spelled ♯4 or ♭5, which are enharmonic equivalents. The most likely concept will be in chord substitution studies, but in the case of symmetrical diminished there's plenty of tritone fodder to explore.

It's *not* a Diminished Scale

I learned about the two main octatonic scales from Wayne Krantz. At the heart of his methodology is the emphasis on formula and training yourself to make it work for your playing in real time, all the time. When he introduced octatonic scales, it was made clear to me there were two closely related, yet distinctly different, diminished-based scales. Both were symmetrical in makeup, but the one whose formula was perfectly suited for sophisticated playing over dominant chords was the one that utilized the term "symmetrical" in its name. The other one was just the "diminished scale" or the "whole/half scale." While the diminished scale follows a pattern of repeating step sequences, the formula—1 2 ♭3 4 ♭5 #5 6 7—leaves little question as to its probable application. Looking at the diminished scale's formula from a slightly more revealing perspective, it becomes even clearer: 1 9 ♭3 4 ♭5 #5 ♭♭7 7. While there is a tritone between the 3rd and one of the 7th degrees (♭♭7), it is not the one in a dominant seventh chord. Conversely, it's from a... wait for it... a diminished seventh chord!

THE SYMMETRICAL FACTOR

When it comes to scale names, we have two more to justify—double diminished and, well, symmetrical diminished! To fully understand why symmetrical diminished is named as such, you have to understand what constitutes musical symmetry and possess a familiarity with fully diminished harmony principles.

Musical Symmetry

The term "symmetry," put simply, refers to something made up of equal parts. The collection of equal parts in the case of this scale all result from the repeating cycle of alternating half steps and whole steps as discussed earlier. Those repeating parts, built off each scale degree, are as follows:

- minor 3rd intervals

- augmented 4th/♭5th intervals, also referred to as tritones

- major 6th intervals

- diminished arpeggios

- fully diminished seventh arpeggios

In fact, the entire scale is equal to itself allowing any given fingering to move up or down the neck and still be the same scale, just with a different note order. For example, the C symmetrical diminished scale that kicked off this chapter can move up or down a minor 3rd (three frets) and still be the same scale, just with different starting and ending degrees. It is these qualities that put the symmetry in the symmetrical diminished name.

The Original Symmetrical Concept

If you're already familiar with musical symmetry, it's a safe bet your introduction was through fully diminished seventh chords and arpeggios. They, too, contain repeating cyclical elements, such as minor 3rds and tritones, and are also equal to themselves, thus allowing you the same advantageous ease of movement about the neck.

The connection between the symmetrical diminished scale and the fully diminished seventh concept is simple: there are two fully diminished seventh arpeggios nested in a symmetrical diminished scale. One starts from the first note; the other starts from the next note a half step above. With both arpeggios being made up of four notes, you can do the math and see how they equal an octatonic scale! It's for this reason the scale is named with diminished in the title and it also justifies the double diminished scale moniker. In Chapter 3, you'll learn how to best interpret these nested elements, thus making the most of the possibilities they present.

CHORD APPLICATIONS

Before moving forward from this symmetrical diminished primer, let's take a look at all the dominant chord types this scale can be played over (see following note). Conversely, these are also chords that can be constructed from this scale. Take note: you'll notice that the #4/♭5/#11 degree possibilities discussed earlier are represented here.

- dominant seventh
- dominant seventh ♭5
- dominant seventh ♭9
- dominant seventh #9
- dominant seventh #11
- dominant seventh ♭5♭9
- dominant seventh ♭5#9
- dominant seventh ♭9#11
- dominant seventh #9#11
- dominant 13th
- dominant 13th ♭5
- dominant 13th ♭9
- dominant 13th #9
- dominant 13th ♭5♭9
- dominant 13th ♭5#9

Freedom of Symmetry

This list should not in any way strictly dictate when you do or don't use symmetrical diminished to create outside lines. It's here for learning and reference purposes. Playing outside is just that: playing outside the confines of what most people judge as tonal, safe-sounding, and/or continuously pleasing to the ear. The chords listed here are technically what you *could* play symmetrical diminished over, or, to put it another way, are *supposed* to be what you play symmetrical diminished over. To be clear: it is not my intention to impose any artistic barriers to your playing. This is especially true with regards to playing outside. My intentions are firmly rooted in giving you the tools to thoroughly visualize and completely master all the incredible possibilities symmetrical diminished has to offer. Symmetrical concepts have an element of freedom you should explore and consequently run with. With the skills and insight you'll gain from this book, you have only yourself to impose limits on what you can do with this newfound freedom and when to use it. Onward!

CHAPTER 2

VERTICAL FINGERINGS

Now that you have some background information on symmetrical diminished, let's get movin' and groovin' with some fingerings and more lines. In this chapter, we're going to first learn about what's up with my quirky names for scale fingerings as you learn about *Fingering Groups*. The three Groups we're going to look into will all be based on a three-note-per-string approach. In addition to examining these fingerings in their own Groups, you'll have a full-neck vision map to help you begin to master symmetrical diminished all over the fretboard.

In the previous chapter, I gave you a single symmetrical diminished fingering to play—Zig-Zag/Vertical Hybrid Positional #1 (ZZVHP #1)—and a collection of 12 lines to get a feel for what you can do with this amazing scale. You also learned about the powerful and tantalizing musical labyrinth that is musical symmetry. In regards to scales, symmetry creates multiple repeating, cyclical elements that allow you to create amazing sounding and adventurous lines that are just plain fun to play. Over a span of three frets, you could play the same exact fingering and cover changes in all 12 key centers. That is, if you can navigate the shifting scale degree designations.

To become a symmetrical diminished Jedi, you must invest time in studying and mastering approaches to controlling this mighty melodic tool. To begin, it's important to have a system to distinguish repeating symmetrical scale fingerings from one another. For that purpose, I created a naming system that I now pass on to you.

Since symmetrical diminished scales can move up or down 1-1/2 steps (or three frets) and retain the same notes just in a different order, I created Fingering Groups. The three Groups I'm going to show in this chapter are:

- Vertical Positional
- Zig-Zag Positional
- Zig-Zag Vertical Hybrid Positional

To more easily communicate these Group names, I will abbreviate them throughout the book like this:

- **Vertical Positional**: VP
- **Zig-Zag Positional**: ZZP
- **Zig-Zag Vertical Hybrid Positional**: ZZVHP

Following the connection with fully diminished tetrad symmetrical ideology, each Group consists of four scales. Each scale will have a Group name followed by a number designation from 1–4.

VERTICAL POSITIONAL

The *Vertical Positional* (VP) fingering is the most localized in the symmetrical diminished family of fingerings. Here's an example from the root A:

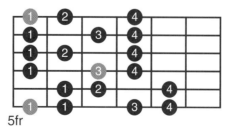

5fr

With the exception of the lowest root on the fifth fret, sixth string, Vertical Positional #1 is a three-note-per-string layout. What's more, the other three VP fingerings in the Group will be strictly three notes per string, which makes for a strong dominant seventh chord association since each of the lowest notes will be the remaining chord tones: 3, 5, and ♭7. Let's look at the scale degree layout more closely in the next section.

Finger Pattern

Because of the symmetrical nature of symmetrical diminished, any vertical, localized fingerings will be part of a group of fingering patterns that repeat. From a three-note-per-string standpoint, there are three groups of identical adjacent string finger patterns. Here they are in Vertical Positional #1:

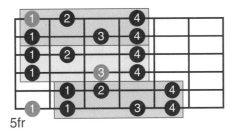

5fr

On the lower of the three adjacent string sets, you have a 1–3–4 fingering for the whole step/half step instance, and on the higher string, you see a 1–2–4 for the inverse (half step/whole step). Its condensed three-fret architecture, and the fact that it repeats throughout the fingering, contributes to the name of the Group as well. This fingering is the quintessential symmetrical diminished finger pattern and will come into play many times over within the various patterns you'll explore later in Chapters 6 and 7.

> **Distinguished Fingerings**
>
> Have you ever noticed certain finger patterns seem to only appear with certain families of scales? If so, good! That's because scales of all types, including symmetrical diminished, contain distinguishing finger patterns. These help you more quickly retain certain scales while giving you a visual picture as to what the functions of their notes are. In Chapter 5, you'll learn how I do this with chords!

Scale Degree Layout

The struggle in weighing the pros and cons of symmetrical repetition is real. One way to make the pros outshine the cons is to put the time into studying the scale degree layout of a given fingering Group and how it shifts from one to the next. This is especially true for the vertical fingering Groups you'll work with throughout this chapter. Let's look at the *Vertical Positional Group* layout with G as the root and all other scale degree distance designations based off of G.

Vertical Positional #1

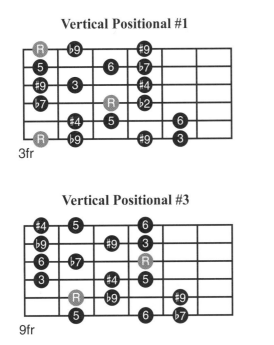

3fr

Vertical Positional #2

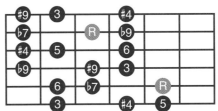

6fr

Vertical Positional #3

3fr

Vertical Positional #4

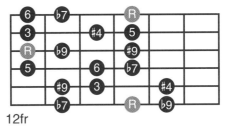

9fr

12fr

There are a few ways to analyze and organize the scale degree designation changes.

- The initial way most guitar players visualize neck location is by the lowest note of either a chord or scale. With regards to the latter, VP #1 starts on the root, VP #2 on the 3, VP #3 on the 5, and finally VP #4 on the ♭7. As noted previously, these starting points follow a dominant seventh chord tone pattern.

- When it comes to constructing great lines, the focus (at first) should be where all the root notes are. You can do that by locating the octave shapes within each fingering. VP #1 contains three root notes that together take on the shape of a (nearly) equilateral triangle going up the neck. VP #2 has a two-fret octave shape based off the fifth string in what I call a "diagonal south" direction, whereas VP #3 has a two-note "diagonal north" octave shape off the fifth string. VP #4 contains three root notes that also take on the shape of a (nearly) equilateral triangle, this time in the opposite direction (going down the neck).

- I find the most effective way to visualize location and connections are by way of chords. This idea will be covered in Chapter 5 and will open up compelling possibilities.

Lines

The following four lines are from the four scales in the Vertical Positional Group in G. Notice how the lines all relate to each other, but at the same time make the necessary shifts relative to the scale degree layout. Also note the resolutions to basic dominant seventh chord tones (G, B, D, or F) while making deliberate use of the three adjacent string pairs. Focus on how these combined attributes shape the line.

Example 13 starts off with ideas on the higher adjacent string of each of the pairs pointed out in the Finger Patterns section. An important line construction technique to be aware of early on is my use of legato and the places where it falls in the rhythm. This helps break up the possible monotonous results that repeating fingering patterns can easily influence and/or breed while helping to give the line rhythmic movement. After playing through the nested diminished seventh arpeggio fragments (those will be covered in Chapter 3) going from bar 1 into bar 2, there's a return to the deliberate use of the string pairs on the D–G and B–E string sets. The line finally resolves on the 5th of the chord.

 *Example 13*

Relative to the idea in the first lick, Example 14 starts off with motives on the lower strings of the adjacent pairs only to return to the higher string leading to the diminished seventh arpeggio fragments. This was done so there was emphasis on chord tones in the starting motives. This is also why the lick concludes in the same manner as Example 13 and also ends on a chord tone—this time the ♭7th.

 *Example 14*

Example 15 returns to Example 13's string assignments for those initial motives but changes the note order on the second one (starting on beat 2) so as not to emphasize the weak-sounding 6th degree. The approach and carrying out of the diminished seventh arpeggios remain the same because of the chord tone content in the arpeggios (more on this in Chapter 3). The final motif starting on beat 3 of bar 2 finds itself on the second and third strings for the first time, allowing a strong finish to the root on the 12th fret (G).

Example 15

Vertical Positional #3

This final lick has no alterations as compared to Example 14 because it sways in the same positive melodic direction when it comes to the frequency and placement of the chord tones. Sometimes it just works out that way!

Example 16

Vertical Positional #4

ZIG-ZAG POSITIONAL

The *Zig-Zag Positional* (ZZP) has an element of back-and-forth movement (as indicated in the name) while still maintaining a vertical feel within a three-note-per-string setup. In congruence with Vertical Positional, here's an example from the root A. Be sure to play and compare the two.

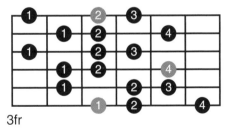

3fr

Finger Pattern

In ZZP #1, you see three groups of another signature repeating adjacent string finger pattern. This time it's a half step/whole step sequence on the lower adjacent string and the inverse on the higher adjacent string.

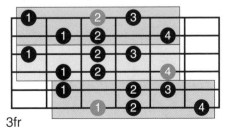

3fr

Notice how the higher adjacent string is a 1–2–3 fingering for a whole step/half step sequence setting up each pair's fret-hand second finger to line up on the same fret. If it seems awkward at first, give it a chance, as it will soon become an advantage when you start playing the line ideas—especially with regards to legato feel.

Scale Degree Layout

Right along with the change in fingering is the feel for the scale degree layout. Let's look at all four:

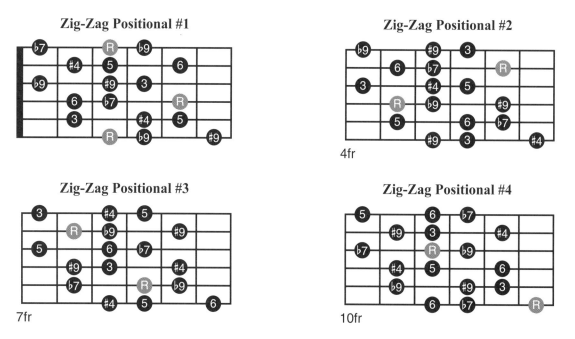

Looking at the ZZP Group you'll notice the same identifiable attributes as in the VP Group with regards to the root. This strengthens the case for chords being the go-to vision tool in visualizing and organizing symmetrical diminished scales up and down the neck. All will be revealed in that regard in Chapter 5.

Lines

Here are another four lines, this time from the four scales in the Zig-Zag Positional Group in G. Following the same parameters as the Vertical Positional Group lines, notice how different the lines feel while still resolving on the root and exploiting the adjacent string pairs.

Example 17 starts off with a rolling legato idea that travels down the highest adjacent string pair and crosses over to the next on beat 3, only to reiterate the legato idea at the same juncture of the adjacent pair on beat 4, this time on the 4–3 string pair. What's to be taken away from that approach is this: even if you choose to focus on adjacent string pairs, they should not create a boundary as to where you can take your idea. The momentary chromatic passage at the beginning of measure 2 (yes, you can add passing tones to symmetrical diminished ideas!) leads up to a 1–3–5 arpeggio that jumps to a slide between the altered lines resolving to the root.

 *Example 17*

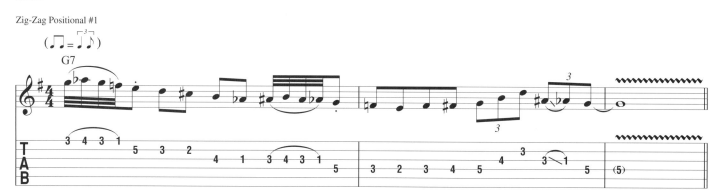

This lick starts off the same and maintains the note order for the entire bar on the potency of the legato element as well as the high concentration of chord tones. However, the eighth-note idea that starts off bar 2 slightly changes so as to allow for a G on the downbeat instead of an A♭ (♭9). There's also no half-step approach tone to the root of the B♭ arpeggio (just because you can add passing tones doesn't always mean you should). After the slide within beat 4, the last note is a bend to the 5th of the chord. Half-step bends are too cool to pass up, especially when they create a tension-and-release passage such as this (♯4 to 5).

Example 18

Zig-Zag Positional #2

Example 19 is the same as Example 17, just up a tritone and with the exception of a bending element as first seen in Example 18. The chord tone balance, the strength of the legato, and the more effective result of the chromatic passage made this a less evasive transformation from the initial ZZP #1-based lick.

Example 19

Zig-Zag Positional #3

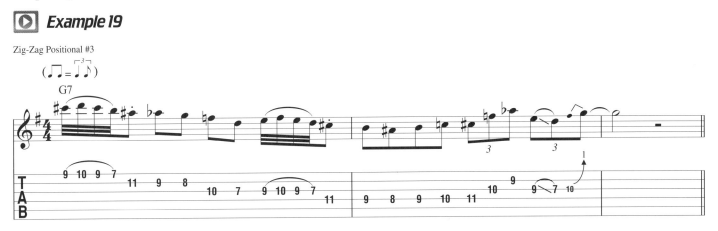

Once again the lick retains the original composition of bar 1 first started in Example 17 for the same reasons: the memorizing effect of the legato and the chord tone placement, as well as the ratio to tension tones. Bar 2 makes the same chromatic movement to superimposed arpeggio, but notice the arpeggio is not major. Instead, it's minor—E minor, to be exact. This is due to the ineffectiveness of major triads built from the 6th degree. In many instances, the pull of the sound strays too far from the intent of the lick, making it sound "wrong." The moral of the story: just because you have symmetrical elements nested in the symmetrical diminished scale at your disposal doesn't mean they'll always work.

Example 20

Zig-Zag Positional #4

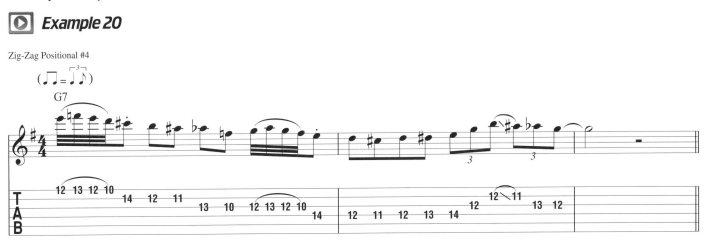

ZIG-ZAG/VERTICAL HYBRID POSITIONAL

The Zig-Zag/Vertical Hybrid Positional fingering is a combination of the first two Groups and was the first symmetrical diminished fingering I laid out for you in Chapter 1, which was followed by a set of lines. The scale degree layout is mapped out between the VP and ZZP Groups. In regards to the adjacent string patterns first introduced in the VP and ZZP Groups, the ZZVHP possesses both patterns and even has an overlapping pattern as a result of the four-note-per-string sequence on the fourth string.

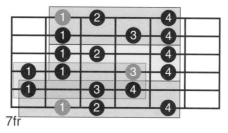

7fr

I Spy More Overlapping
Take a closer look at the VP and ZZP Groups and you may see more examples of adjacent string pattern overlapping.

FULL NECK VISION

With a thorough look into two three-note-per-string symmetrical diminished scale approaches in a vertical position logged in, let's start to look at how we can use them to establish a full neck vision. One way is to combine the Vertical Positional and Zig-Zag Positional Groups into a roadmap of scales that start and end on each degree. Maintaining the Groups' tonal center of G, as seen in this chapter, it would look this:

Zig-Zag Positional #1

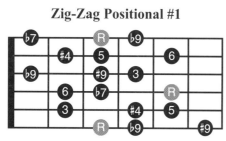

Vertical Positional #1

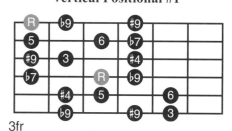

3fr

Zig-Zag Positional #2

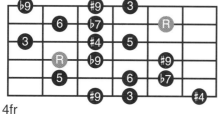

4fr

Vertical Positional #2

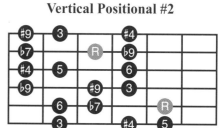

6fr

Zig-Zag Positional #3

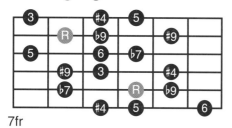

7fr

Vertical Positional #3

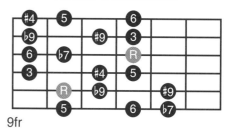

9fr

Zig-Zag Positional #4

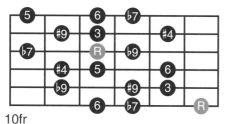

10fr

Vertical Positional #4

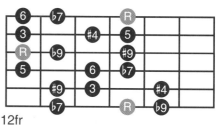

12fr

Mapping out the neck with symmetrical diminished scales can also be done in all 12 keys. Here's a way that will challenge your developing vision, thus helping you take it to the next level. This is a descending run down the neck beginning with a B symmetrical diminished scale in a Vertical Positional #1 fingering starting on the ♭9th degree and ending with the B♭ symmetrical diminished scale in a Zig-Zag Positional #4 fingering. The scales will follow a consistent alternating pattern of VP to ZZP fingerings that will descend in order after the first pair of #1 fingerings. Check it out:

B Symmetrical Diminished
Vertical Positional #1

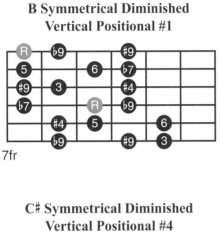

7fr

C Symmetrical Diminished
Zig-Zag Positional #1

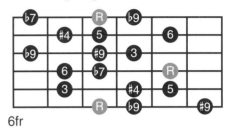

6fr

C♯ Symmetrical Diminished
Vertical Positional #4

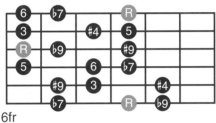

6fr

D Symmetrical Diminished
Zig-Zag Positional #4

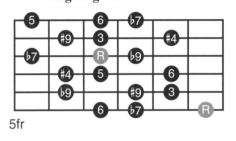

5fr

E♭ Symmetrical Diminished
Vertical Positional #3

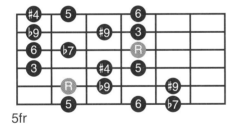

5fr

E Symmetrical Diminished
Zig-Zag Positional #3

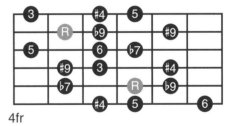

4fr

F Symmetrical Diminished
Vertical Positional #2

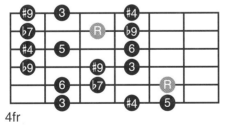

4fr

F♯ Symmetrical Diminished
Zig-Zag Positional #2

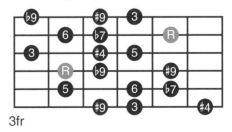

3fr

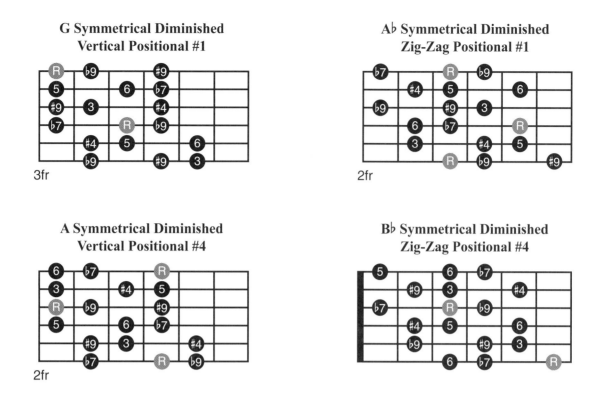

G Symmetrical Diminished
Vertical Positional #1

A♭ Symmetrical Diminished
Zig-Zag Positional #1

A Symmetrical Diminished
Vertical Positional #4

B♭ Symmetrical Diminished
Zig-Zag Positional #4

One way to identify with these descending fingerings is to play the lines I've provided in this chapter and match them to the corresponding scale where it's applicable. Take note: you'll need to transpose them to make that work.

When playing through both of these neck visions, be sure to stay focused on alternating between the two fingering types. The more time you dedicate to training yourself to quickly identify and implement the scale degree layout, the more successful you'll be with keeping it all together. In Chapter 5, you'll learn another way to visualize the neck through altered harmonic connections, but first Chapter 3 is going to take you through a trio of nested symmetrical intervals and a pair of fully diminished seventh arpeggios.

CHAPTER 3
NESTED SYMMETRICAL COMPONENTS

Throughout the first two chapters, you played through several collections of lines—most with specific themes and focus points. In the next two chapters, we're going to embark on a two-part expedition to strengthen your command of symmetrical diminished scales, as well as your visualization of them. In this chapter, you will play through a symmetrical diminished boot camp by way of nested intervallic and arpeggio-based activities. The idea is to ring in some of the ideas seen thus far and to be able to better use them in your composing and playing of outside lines with symmetrical diminished. To do this, we're going to chop up the Vertical Positional and Zig-Zag Positional Group scales and play them in various directions. Knowledge is power, and so is time spent on neck vision, chops, and mastery of a chosen melodic device.

NESTED SYMMETRICAL INTERVALS

A great tool for coming up with outside lines of your own with any scale is the intervallic approach. The challenge is the varying shapes you have to coordinate and become familiar with due to the varying types of intervals (major vs. minor, perfect vs. diminished and/or augmented), as well as inconsistency in standard tuning with regards to the G and B string. One way to quickly unlock this potential is discovering if a scale has nested symmetrical intervals. This provides you with a higher ratio of consistent shapes, making it easier and quicker to get them under your fingers.

Inside every symmetrical diminished scale is a trio of nested symmetrical intervals. They are:

- minor 3rds
- tritones
- major 6ths

In the following sections, you're going to play the Vertical Positional and Zig-Zag Positional fingerings chopped up in each of the three nested symmetrical interval possibilities.

Symmetrical Diminished Work Order
You're about to play through three different intervallic scalar approaches: Basic Directions, Turnarounds, and Alternates. There are two ways to play each approach. You'll find one approach per interval for both fingering types, making four intervallic nuggets to play for each interval, totaling 12 exercises in all. Be sure to loop each exercise a few times, as that confirms your command and control. Once you get a handle on the concepts, it's up to you to apply all three approaches, not only to the remaining scales in each of the Groups, but also to all 12 keys, as well as the other scale fingering types you'll learn later in the book. What sounds like a lot of work is not as much as you think. The form and consistency born of musical symmetry will make endeavors such as this more efficient, productive, and fun!

Minor 3rds
The first nested symmetrical interval used to slice and dice the VP and ZZP fingering types is the minor 3rd (♭3rd). The concept applied is called *Basic Directions*, where you'll play the interval pairs in the same direction as you ascend and descend the scale fingerings. In the first Direction, Forward-Forward, you'll play a scale degree followed by the intended interval. So, the pitch direction will be low to high, hence the "forward" direction. After playing both fingering types, you'll switch to the opposite approach, called Backward-Backward, where the picture direction will now be high to low, or in a "backward" direction.

Example 21

Vertical Positional Forward-Forward ♭3rds

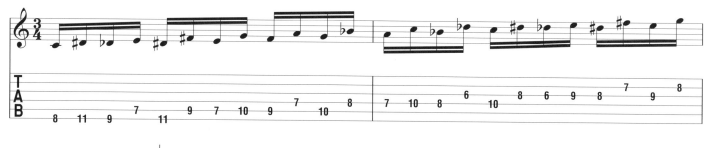

Example 22

Zig-Zag Positional Forward-Forward ♭3rds

Example 23

Vertical Positional Backward-Backward ♭3rds

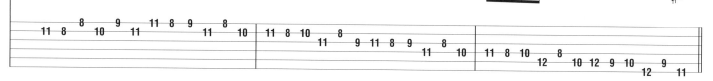

Example 24

Zig-Zag Positional Backward-Backward ♭3rds

If you're having difficulty looping these, feel free to change the parameters: slow the tempo down, alter the rhythms, or insert a bar of rest before starting over. I encourage you to mix it up. It's great for your practicing, your musicality, and—let's be honest—your sanity!

> **Fingering Disclosure**
> The Vertical Positional scales throughout these next three sections were assembled without the initial half step sequence as seen in VP #1. This was done to keep a consistent three-note-per-string vision and timing feel going from one fingering type to the next.

Tritones

The next nested symmetrical interval to be applied to the scalar chopping block is the tritone (♯4th or ♭5th). You'll explore this nested interval through C and F♯ symmetrical diminished scales, which are separated by a tritone as well. The sequencing concept applied here is called *Turnarounds*, where you'll play the interval pairs in one direction as you ascend, and then the opposite as you descend. The switch is made after playing the pair that includes the highest note of the fingering. Be aware that will vary from VP to ZZP.

Example 25

Vertical Positional Forward-Backward Tritones

Example 26

Zig-Zag Positional Forward-Backward Tritones

Example 27

Vertical Positional Backward-Forward Tritones

Example 28

Zig-Zag Positional Backward-Forward Tritones

Major 6ths

The third and final nested symmetrical interval employed to break up the VP and ZZP fingerings will be the major 6th. This time around, I used a concept called *Alternates*, where the direction of the intervals is alternated one after another as you ascend and descend each fingering. For example, in Forward Alternate, you'll start with a low-to-high note pair, which, in this case, will be root to 6th. The next pair will be a high-to-low pair: ♭7th and ♭9th. To check yourself, look for certain things to happen. For example, the pair that contains the highest note will always be in the opposite direction of the starting pair. The same goes for the pair you play at the end before looping around to the beginning again.

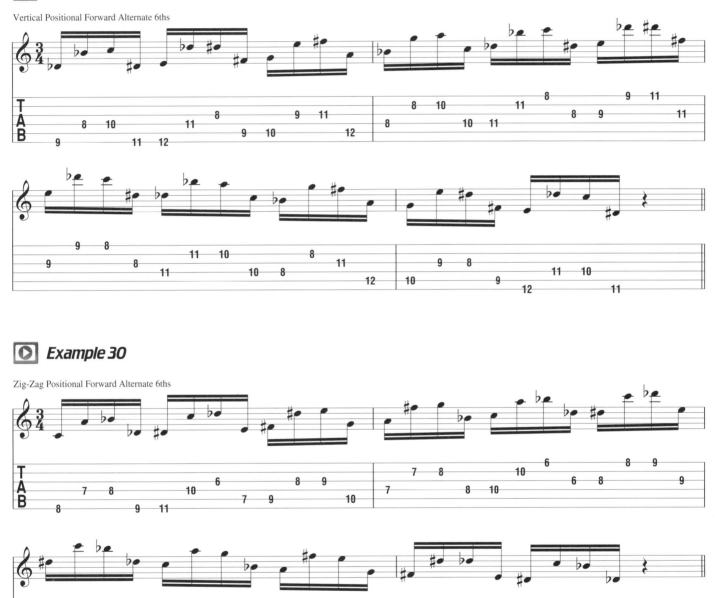

Example 29

Vertical Positional Forward Alternate 6ths

Example 30

Zig-Zag Positional Forward Alternate 6ths

Example 31

Vertical Positional Backward Alternate 6ths

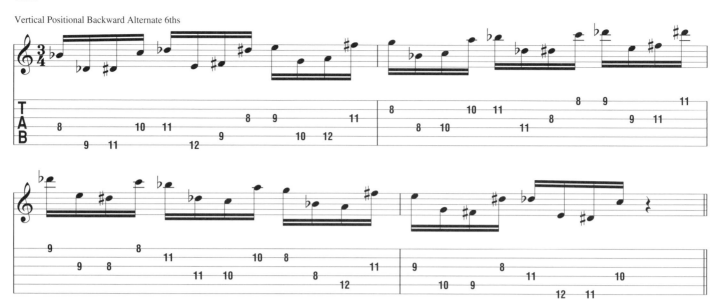

Example 32

Zig-Zag Positional Backward Alternate 6ths

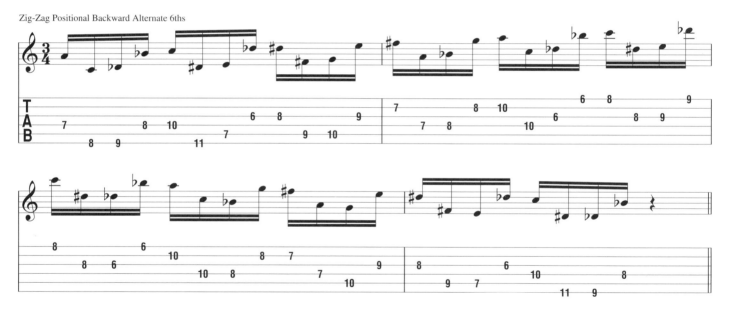

NESTED DIMINISHED SEVENTH ARPEGGIOS

As you learned in Chapter 1, there is a pair of fully diminished seventh arpeggios nested in the symmetrical diminished scale, whose combined chord tones account for all eight notes in this octatonic scale. They also are the basis for one of the alternative names used for symmetrical diminished: double diminished. In the following sections, you'll learn about their specific functions and how best to use them. You'll see how two six-string diminished seventh arpeggio shapes fit into both Vertical Positional and Zig-Zag Positional, which will be supported by exercises for you to shed.

Direct Diminished

The diminished tetrad built from the symmetrical diminished scale root is what I call *direct diminished* because of its direct correlation. To see how this works, first look at a C symmetrical diminished scale:

$$C \quad D\flat \quad D\# \quad E \quad F\# \quad G \quad A \quad B\flat$$

Extract its odd numbered notes (minor 3rds), and you have the direct diminished seventh chord tones:

$$C \quad E\flat \quad F\#(G\flat) \quad A(B\flat\flat)$$

Played over a C7 or corresponding C7 altered, the arpeggio will have an aggressive, Dorian-esque minor blues effect, since you're playing the following symmetrical diminished scale degrees over the chord:

Root
#9 (or ♭3)
#4 (or ♭5)
6 (or ♭♭7)

Nested Direct Diminished Seventh Arpeggio Shapes

So far, you've looked at everything directly from the perspective of a symmetrical diminished scale. The two diminished seventh arpeggio shapes seen here will be presented in relation to a six-string C7 arpeggio in the 8th position:

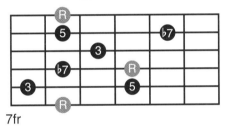

C7 Arpeggio - Root Position

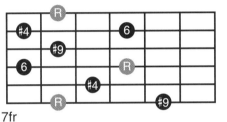

Direct Diminished 7th Arpeggio - Scalene Right

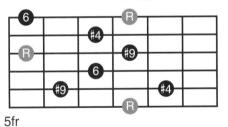

Direct Diminished 7th Arpeggio - Scalene Left

Each diminished seventh tetrad arpeggio is made up of symmetrical minor 3rds. Grouped in three-note-per adjacent string pairs—E/A, D/G, B/E—they take on the shape of a scalene triangle. Notice in Scalene Right, the head of the triangle faces right, while in Scalene Left it faces left. Also notice Scalene Right is more vertically positioned as compared to Scalene Left. As for fingering, I suggest going with a 1–4–2 for Scalene Right and a 3–1–4 for Scalene Left.

Nested Direct Diminished Seventh Arpeggio Exercises

Instead of putting time into playing the arpeggios outside of the symmetrical diminished scale, the following exercises will have you weaving them in and out of both the Vertical Positional and Zig-Zag Positional fingerings. The first exercise is a C symmetrical diminished scale in a Zig-Zag Positional #1; you start off ascending the scale in bar 1 and then descend a nested Scalene Right direct diminished arpeggio shape in bar 2. This will be followed by the inverse for each idea: the scale will then descend in bar 3 while the arpeggio ascends in bar 4. Take note of the repeating note that occurs when making the transition from bar 3 to bar 4.

▶ *Example 33*

Next up is a C symmetrical diminished in a Vertical Positional #1 fingering, sans root, played in the same fashion with regards to scale and arpeggio direction. In bar 1, the scale ascends to its highest note and proceeds to descend a Scalene Left direct diminished arpeggio in bar 2. Bars 3 and 4 will flip the direction of the scale and arpeggio once again with an ascending Scalene Right dominant diminished arpeggio capping it off.

▶ *Example 34*

The Shape of Chords to Come
With diminished seventh arpeggios come diminished seventh chords. In Chapter 5, you're going to discover how to use chord shapes to visualize the symmetrical diminished scale and its degrees, helping make your symmetrical diminished vision that much stronger and thus making your line construction that much more effective.

Dominant Diminished

A half step above the symmetrical diminished scale root is the beginning of the *dominant diminished* tetrad arpeggio. As a result, the dominant diminished chord tones are all a half step above any direct diminished chord tones.

Db(C#)   E   G   Bb

Played over a C7 or corresponding C7 altered, the arpeggio will have a curried 7b9 sound as you play the following symmetrical diminished scale degrees over the chord:

b9
3
5
b7

Notice every note of that diminished seventh arpeggio is a C7 chord tone with the exception of the root, which is the b9 of C7. This is the basis for the #iv°7 approach in the blues.

Nested Dominant Diminished Seventh Arpeggio Shapes

The next two diminished seventh arpeggio shapes will again be presented in relation to a six-string C7 arpeggio in the eighth position, but this time, since they're dominant diminished, they're a half step higher. Be sure to examine and analyze the correlating symmetrical diminished scale tone degrees in all four arpeggios.

C7 Arpeggio - Root Position

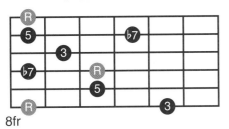

Dominant Diminished 7th Arpeggio - Scalene Right

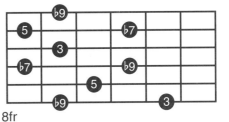

Dominant Diminished 7th Arpeggio - Scalene Left

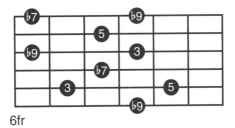

Nested Dominant Diminished Seventh Arpeggio Exercises

Continuing to weave nested diminished arpeggios within the VP and ZZP fingerings, the following exercise will have you descending and ascending a Scalene Left dominant diminished seventh arpeggio nested in the same C symmetrical diminished scale in a Zig-Zag Positional #1 fingering. Watch for the repeating b9's going from bar 1 into bar 2.

▶ **Example 35**

The final exercise will start off ascending a C symmetrical diminished scale in a Vertical Positional #1 fingering, again sans root, that flows right into a Scalene Right dominant diminished seventh arpeggio. Bars 3 and 4 will have you switching directions. Similar to the previous run, watch for the repeating ♭9's, this time going from bar 3 to bar 4, which are at the bottom of the scale.

▶ **Example 36**

Besides the chops benefits, these exercises shine a light on the patterns of what arpeggio types are in what fingerings. Check it out:

- **ZZP Direct Diminished**: Scalene Right
- **ZZP Dominant Diminished**: Scalene Left
- **VP Direct Diminished**: Scalene Left
- **VP Dominant Diminished**: Scalene Right

In Chapter 4, we'll return to playing lines. Following the lines at the onset, which make use of the nested symmetrical intervals discussed at the beginning of this chapter, there will also be the use of the two types of these nested diminished seventh arpeggios. What's more, the lines will guide you through the many possibilities of Scalene Right and Left arpeggio shapes applied to direct and dominant diminished, and not just based off the root (direct diminished) and ♭9 (dominant diminished) degrees as seen in this chapter. From there, you'll play through a bevy of symmetrical diminished lines that are shaped to resolve to a tonic, paving the way for you to play over changes!

CHAPTER 4
LINE CONSTRUCTION AND APPLICATION

With a return to playing lines, the next two sections will showcase outside lines that make use of the symmetrical components learned in Chapter 3. You'll find a gaggle of themes throughout this collection, including shifting in and out of outside sounds, nested intervals, diminished seventh arpeggios, chord tone resolution, a concept called permutation, and even a lick called a "ricochet!" Additionally, there will be conceptual advice tidbits spread all over, which are just as important as the notes and the theory. The lines will be organized in various neck visions made up of the VP and ZZP Fingering Groups, providing a thorough symmetrical diminished examination.

STATIC IMPROVISATION

When it comes to improvisation, the term *static* refers to improvising over or within the confines of one element—whether that element is played at the same time or not. An example everyone can relate to—and presumably has logged in countless hours participating in—is the infamous one-chord jam. In many instances, that one chord is a dominant seventh chord of some type, straight or altered to some degree. Weaving in and out of inside and outside lines will give your improvisations more depth and allow you to have more to say. The trick is being creative, careful, and in command of your outside lines no matter how frequent and "out" they are.

Symmetrical Interval Approaches

The following eight lines focus on weaving in and out of symmetrical diminished ideas that have nested symmetrical 3rds, tritones, and 6ths. You'll play through a complete set of both the Vertical Positional and Zig-Zag Positional Groups, albeit in varying keys. Be mindful of each line's content so you can continue developing your scale degree layout awareness with regards to this complex scale.

Starting things off in E♭ within an 11th-position E♭7 arpeggio, the first line slides into a ZZP #1 fingering at beat 3 and proceeds to ascend adjacent string pairs on the G–B and D–G string sets. Notice how the second sequence is slightly offset with syncopation and serves to anticipate the second bar. Rhythmic tension is resolved on the upbeat of 1 with an ascending run on symmetrical diminished forward 3rds that climaxes with a half-step approach bend to the 5th.

▶ Example 37

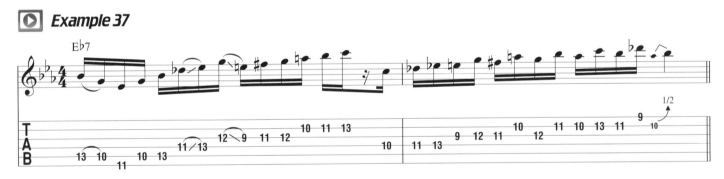

The next line is played over a static A7 or qualifying A7 altered chord and starts with a descending A Mixolydian idea. At beat 4 in bar 1, the direction of the Mixolydian idea reverses to set up a descending alternating sequence of symmetrical 6ths down the VP #1 A symmetrical diminished scale. The tension resolves at beat 3, bar 2 with a triad fragment vision of chord tones that sets up a unison bend to the 5th.

▶ Example 38

The ZZP #2 line in F makes effective use of ascending tritone octave groups off the 3rd, 5th, and root before flowing into a descent down an F7 arpeggio peppered with a slur from the minor 3rd to major 3rd for a tasteful bluesy feel. The effect of rapid-fire symmetrical tritones played in this manner makes for a cool, almost bubbling sound that always delivers, but it's even more effective when simmered with a more inside-sounding exit.

Example 39

In an 11th-position B dominant environment, the line sets up adjacent string-set playing with inside triplet-based ideas on beats 1 and 2. The triplet feel continues, as does the adjacent string approach, with a symmetrical fingering that takes the line outside, within the confines of VP #2. The one-up, one-down triplet motif continues into bar 2, beat 1 and helps bridge the outside element to an inside 16th-note flurry in B Mixolydian that ends on the 3rd.

Example 40

Using 6ths from the start, this line in A♭ makes its way to a ZZP #3 via an eighth-position A♭ major arpeggio sliced into its own diatonic 6th and minor 3rd. The released bend to a pull-off segues to the symmetrical diminished element, where a brief run on alternating 6ths ascends only to make a jump down to a tritone between the defining 3rd and ♭7th degrees.

Example 41

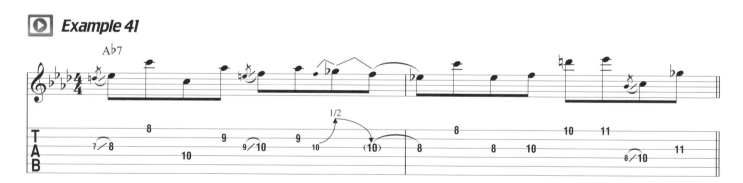

Starting out in D symmetrical diminished VP #3, there's a six-note adjacent string sequence that starts on beat 1 at the #4 on the B–E string set before shifting down to the D–G string set for the same run off the 6th. At the upbeat of beat 3, symmetrical intervallic firepower comes in the form of descending tritones whose last note (#9) slides up to the target chord's (D7) 3rd (F#) on beat 1, bar 2. From there, the line weaves in (descending D major arpeggio) and out (descending symmetrical 3rds) and finally back inside, ending on the 3rd of the chord.

Example 42

In Bb, a ZZP #4 is low on the neck, but not before making a gutsy ascending run based on a first-inversion Bb major chord shape on the 5–4–3 string set, preceding a chromatic walk-up to the 3rd, to start the line off with an inside-sounding vibe. After flowing through more Mixolydian-specific degrees on beat 2, the phrasing shifts from 16ths to triplet eighths, adding to the effects of the outside element entering by way of the ZZP #4 fingering starting on the #4th. The three-note-per-string sequence goes up and then down on the next adjacent string, giving what could be a less exciting symmetrical diminished run more content. This tension is briefly resolved on the downbeat of bar 2 with a Bb7 arpeggio shape on the top strings, only to go outside again on beat 2. That tension is resolved with a backward tritone that serves up a root degree for a solid resolution.

Example 43

Working off the VP #4 fingering in E, the in and out weaving is at every beat throughout bar 1. The idea is based on common shapes and common tones, where a three-note triplet eighth-note inside idea is permutated (more on that concept later) with a symmetrical diminished element to take it outside. In bar 2, the bottom two notes of the three-note motif go out via symmetrical diminished, breaking off into a 16th-note feel starting with a four-note half-step idea on beat 3. The line stays outside and uses the 6th and ♭7th degrees as offset pedal tones through bar 3 until the upbeat of beat 3 where you see that half-step idea return on the higher adjacent string set. The tension is finally resolved after a tritone sets up the root with a 5th-root cadence on the downbeat of bar 4.

Example 44

Diminished Seventh Arpeggio Approaches

The next eight lines focus on weaving in and out of both types of nested symmetrical diminished seventh arpeggios. Take notice of the chromatic descending order of the scales as they run down the neck beginning with B in a Vertical Positional #1 fingering starting on the ♭9th degree. This approach is taken directly from the second full neck vision map you discovered in Chapter 2, where the scales follow a consistent descent of alternating VP and ZZP patterns as they ascend chromatically.

The first line grabs you right away by making use of both dominant and direct diminished seventh arpeggios within VP #1 fingering for B symmetrical diminished. Starting with an ascending middle-string Scalene Right dominant diminished fragment off the ♭7, the line morphs immediately into a descending Scalene Left direct diminished arpeggio of the same fashion starting from the ♯4. This happens again at the juncture going from the first bar to the next, albeit from a different degree. This is a key approach and important to explore right from the start, as it will prove to be a consistently effective way to use both types of diminished seventh arpeggios without sounding predictable or too pattern-like. Note the cool use of descending nested major 6th intervals right before the bluesy finale.

Example 45

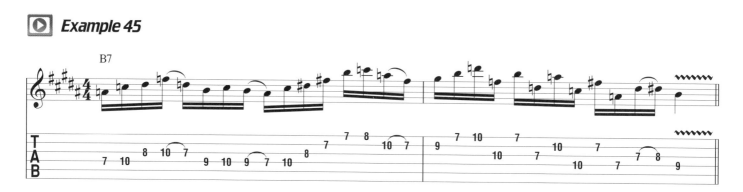

This C symmetrical diminished ZZP-based line kicks off with a descending Scalene Right dominant diminished arpeggio in triplets that transitions to a Scalene Left direct diminished motif, resolving to the 5th of the scale. Don't hesitate to sweep the direct diminished fragment at the downbeat of the second bar and also apply some vibrato to the last note when it feels right. Remember, what you do in practice is what you do in performance. Play as if it counts all the time, and it will!

Example 46

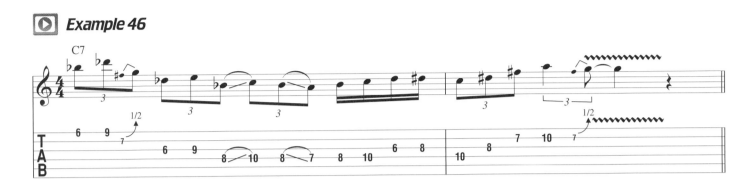

Example 47 is set in a C♯ symmetrical diminished VP #4 scale and makes a blazing run up a Scalene Right dominant diminished arpeggio that segues into a descending run with strategic legato inflections. The line concludes with a brief, yet potent Scalene Left direct diminished fragment. This may be the most vital part of the line, as it introduces you to the gutsy-sounding power of direct diminished over its parallel dominant chord accompaniment.

Example 47

Going with an initial inside sound, this line in D makes use of a seventh-position D major pentatonic scale for the first two beats before making a half step slide down to the #4. From there, you're in a Scalene Left direct diminished arpeggio, hop-scotching up the scale via nested minor 3rds. This is another example of how to effectively use direct diminished as a guttural outside alternative to inside-sounding Mixolydian melodies—great tension-and-release fodder in those one chord jams. At the upbeat of beat 4 in the first bar and for the rest of the line, the diminished seventh arpeggio focus shifts to dominant diminished starting with a half-step bend to ♭9. This makes a full circle return to the vibe originally created at the onset.

Example 48

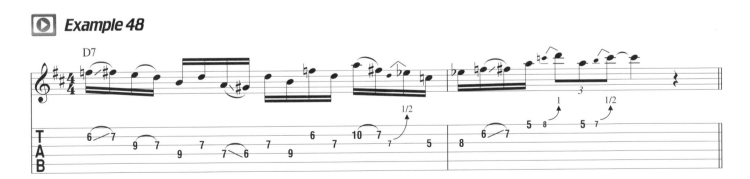

Descending a VP #3 in E♭, the first diminished seventh arpeggio appears at the downbeat of beat 3 with a descending dominant diminished arpeggio. The switch to direct diminished is a clean one at the start of bar 2, but it's the interval that throws the curve ball. The ♭7 from the dominant diminished drops a major 3rd to the #4 of the direct diminished, giving off a different flavor as opposed to the usual onslaught of minor 3rds. The function of direct diminished in this line is purely angular and helps provide an almost Lydian dominant sound when resolved to the E♭ major arpeggio. Keep the existence of that scalar relationship close, as it will come up again and again.

▶ *Example 49*

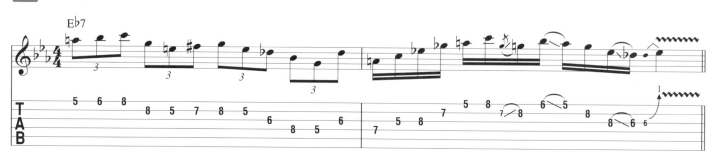

Example 50 shows how even a short line can still squeeze in both types of diminished seventh arpeggios with great effect. Based in an E symmetrical diminished ZZP #3, the line starts with a direct diminished arpeggio that climaxes with a whole-step bend from ♭9 to #9. The angst is resolved with a less tense dominant diminished arpeggio fragment that solidly resolves to the root.

▶ *Example 50*

Direct diminished is not the only way to give your lines some grit. Just listen to the first beat of this line, where a dominant diminished arpeggio fragment is flavored with a half-step bend to the ♭9th and released, followed by a pull-off to the ♭7th resolving on the 5th. This is happening within an F symmetrical diminished VP #2 fingering that moves forward with some nested minor 3rds before mutating the diminished flavor to direct diminished. The descending three-note sequences resolve to a bluesy slur from ♭3 to 3 followed by some syncopated flair.

▶ *Example 51*

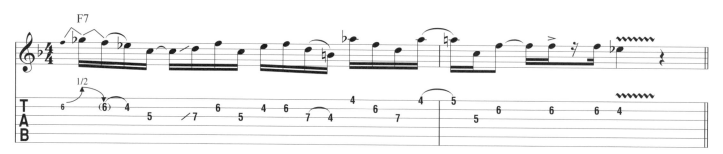

The final diminished seventh line blasts out of the gate with nested tritones that work their way up in various directions to an Yngwie-esque descending dominant diminished arpeggio whose sole purpose is to set up the bend-and-release motif at the downbeat of bar 2. This is purposely reminiscent of what happens at the start of the previous lick. The goal is to show you how the same lick idea can achieve multiple vibes based on their scale degree content. Following that lick is a transference of diminished seventh arpeggio flavor from dominant to direct where you see a descending chromatic run from #9 to root that flows into a ringing major 2nd cluster made up of ♭7 and 1 for a sturdy-sounding final note. It is the sound of 2nds that fuels a very cool advanced concept you'll learn about in the last chapter. Just wait!

 **Example 52**

PLAYING OVER CHANGES

The goal of every improviser is to play over changes. It's a lifelong journey full of thrilling victories and sometimes agonizing defeats. What both moments have in common is the creative journey we all can't get enough of. Much like extreme sports enthusiasts, we're addicted to that rush!

A great way to enhance the excitement of playing over changes is to start adding some outside line ideas to your V chords for some hip-sounding tension and release. What better tool than symmetrical diminished? To help ensure more victory and less defeat, what you need to learn about and exhaustively work on are not only great-sounding outside lines, but also consistently great-sounding resolution points. For every great outside-sounding lick is an even greater inside-sounding escape plan. Say it with me: "You always need an escape plan." Get it? Got it. Good.

This collection is made up of lines that resolve to the target tonic chord by way of its root, 3rd, 5th, and two possible types of 7ths. All the lines will be two bars long and follow a consistent approach. The first bar will be played over the dominant (V) chord, which can be a dominant seventh or a qualifying altered dominant seventh chord (see Chapter 1 for a full list), while the second bar will be the appropriate tonic. With regards to the symmetrical diminished part of the line, this is the first time you're playing through one-bar lines, which is a challenge in itself. Watch how the lines will go from lightly seasoned to totally smothered in symmetrical diminished, all the while maintaining focus on the resolution. Without that, a train wreck is inevitable.

As always, there will be commentary preceding every lick to help you best understand what's packed in the line for you to learn from, as well as the thought behind it. Be sure to pay attention to the most crucial element—the juncture between the symmetrical diminished line and the resolving note. Take notice of the interval separating the two notes, as well as the phrasing.

Starting with a cadence from B7 to E, the key centers will flow chromatically up as you descend down the neck. The procession of tonal centers is once again following the alternating pattern of VP to ZZP fingerings seen in the roadmap laid out for you in Chapter 2 in the Full Neck Vision section, but this time it starts a tritone higher on the neck, allowing an uninterrupted, continuous stream of 24 keys down the neck. That's five sections of 24 lines in all! How's that for a neck vision workout?

Key Signature Heads Up
While the following 24 lines will be shaped as cadences, be aware the key signatures will be tied to the V chord and not the tonic. This is to allow for consistency with regards to the alterations seen in the notation.

Resolving to Tonic Chord Root

The following four lines use symmetrical diminished to create simple tension-and-release resolutions to the tonic chord's root. Pay attention to each line's vibe and see how they attempt to match the intended chord type it resolves to.

In the first line, following the root and 5th degrees played on the first beat, it walks up a B symmetrical diminished scale in a VP #3 fingering only to make a short drop to the ♭9 before resolving to an E major chord's root by way of a whole-step bend on the downbeat of bar 2.

Example 53

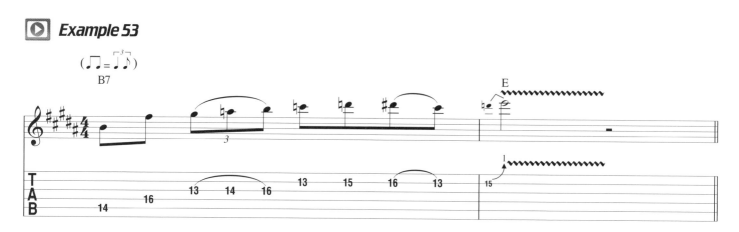

Employing slides, legato, and a half-step bend, this C symmetrical diminished line makes a two-part journey to the Fm resolution. The parts are separated by a tied root note played on the upbeat of beat 2 before the 16th-note motif that ends with a descending half step from the #4 (F#) to the F root. Half-step connections from symmetrical diminished to a resolving chord's destination make for a smooth-sounding line.

Example 54

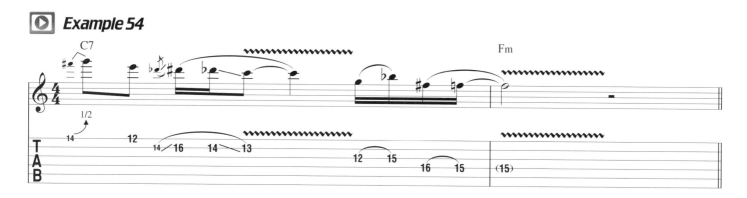

This C# symmetrical diminished run in VP #2 is dressed with descending, forward-motion minor 3rds that resolve to the F#7 root by way of a single-string unison bend. Like the previous line, both pull in the resolution with a 16th-note anticipation. Along with good melodic voice leading, anticipations help make your lines more seasoned and legit.

Example 55

Ascending forward-motion 6ths played in triplets make up the first of the two parts of this D symmetrical diminished line based out of ZZP #2 fingering. Just like Example 55, the second half is played with 16th notes. Think of this as a rhythmic sling shot where the line starts out slow—much like pulling back on the rubber—and ends with a flurry of notes, as if you let it go and made the shot.

Example 56

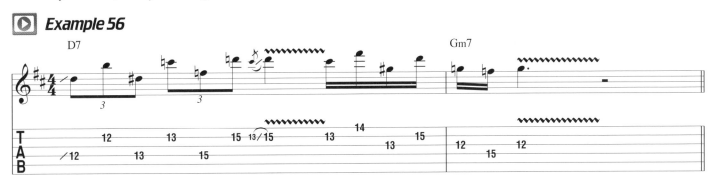

Note the resolution on all four of the previous lines has a little something going on, whether it is a bend, an antici-pation, or a little more than just a single resolving note. The intention is to remind you that the lines you construct needn't be sterile even in these early stages. Always strive to be creative and work towards what you want to sound like. Once again: what you do in practice is what you will sound like in performance. Rest assured, this approach will continue for the rest of these resolving lines.

Resolving to Tonic Chord 3rd

Throughout the next eight lines, you'll find symmetrical diminished being used to resolve to a triad, a dominant seventh, or a major seventh chord's major 3rd, four of which are a quartet of lines derived from a complete set of Vertical Positional fingerings directly related to each other. The purpose is to turn you onto an important concept called *permutations*. When evaluating the resolution chords listed in the charts, keep in mind that basic dominant seventh and major seventh chords can be considered equivalents to extended chords such 9ths, ♯11ths, and 13ths, or any combination thereof.

Here is the first of four lines that are intentionally related to each other. Set in E♭ symmetrical diminished VP #1, it has a root-position minor blues vibe with the exception of the major 3rd played on the upbeat of beat 2. This is one of my go-to symmetrical diminished lick ideas that I use as a launch pad to permute (more on that in Example 59). For now, just rock this line to the resolving major 3rd in A♭.

Example 57

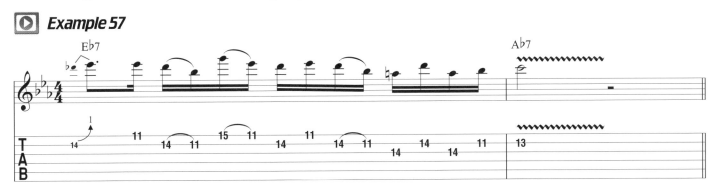

Starting off with a simple descending 5–3–1 E major arpeggio, the symmetrical diminished component kicks in at the fourth 16th of beat 1 with the 6th degree (C♯) of an E symmetrical diminished scale in ZZP #1 fingering. It travels up the scale all the way to the ♭9 before making a grace-note slide into the root (E) a half step below. This sets up a descending minor 3rd drop to the resolving 3rd (C♯) of an Amaj7.

Example 58

In Example 57, you played through one of my favorite VP-based lick ideas. In addition to sounding very cool, it's perfect for altering by way of permutations, which are slight changes made to melodies that can be applied either in a movable (different position) or stationary (same position) fashion. In this case, it's movable, and the tweaks are a shorter initial bend and a resolution that's anticipated by an eighth note with a whole-step bend to the resolving B♭7's 3rd (D). The shorter bend is to counter the weakness of the 6th degree of F symmetrical diminished (D) produced by the whole-step bend, as opposed to Example 57's initial bend to the E♭7 root, which is much more stable and commanding as a starting note. On the flip side, the final bend is the resolution and thus phrased in a way that gives it the spotlight it deserves.

 **Example 59**

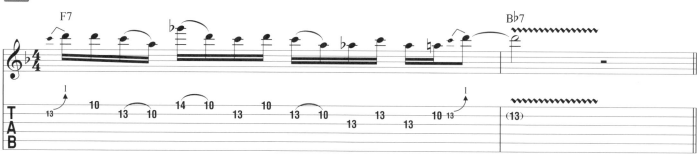

Bringing in a diminished seventh element in the second half of the first bar, this F♯ symmetrical diminished line runs through a ZZP #4 fingering before anticipating the B7's 3rd on the upbeat of beat 4 and then reiterating it in the next bar with a pedal steel-influenced phrase of back-to-back whole-step bends. Check out the unison slide to the #9 on beat 2. While it steps out of the fingering position, that's by no means a bad thing. In fact, a more horizontal approach to your line-playing should be your goal as your symmetrical diminished neck vision develops.

 **Example 60**

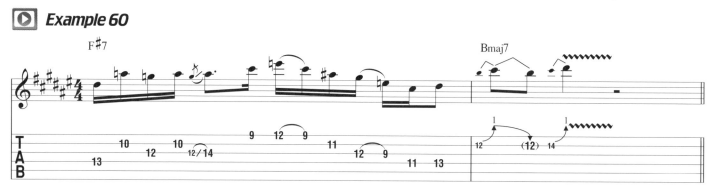

To Resolve to a Minor 3rd or Not to Resolve to a Minor 3rd?
In the words of modern day poets Anthrax, the answer is "Not!" Here's why: as you know, minor 3rds give us minor chords of many types, none of which make a good match with symmetrical diminished. While the symmetrical diminished scale possesses tension tones well suited for setting up a minor chord resolution—take ♭9 and 3 for instance—there are other tones that prevent a strong and convincing cadence.

First, there's the 6th degree of the symmetrical diminished scale. That same note in a resolving minor chord of any type would be the major 3rd! Including that flavor in the dominant chord role makes for a very soggy-sounding cadence that just feels like a wet sock. While I've previously mentioned the value of half-step movement making for good melodic voice leading, it wasn't meant to imply a blanket license for you to drive just any half-step movement past the finish line. Lower the 6th degree, and you're in Phrygian Dominant and Altered scale territory, giving you the goods for some seriously great-sounding minor chord cadences. But, that's another book…

The other rain cloud in symmetrical diminished is the #9, which is a minor 3rd in extended interval/degree sheep's clothing. Once again this is a half-step situation not in your favor, this time contained within symmetrical diminished itself. The half step nearness of #9 and the major 3rd in your lines over dominant chords setting up a minor chord creates a nauseous-sounding cadence that's very likely to fall short in all types of minor chord resolutions.

Continuing with permutations on the line established in Example 57, this G symmetrical diminished line in VP #3 form aims for a C7 resolution with its 3rd (E) as the target tone. Once again, you see a quick bend at the onset and for the same reason—this time to avoid giving the #4 note too much time to overly sour the line right out of the gate. The line takes it home with a minor-3rd pull-off (G to E) to the target tone for a solid finish.

Example 61

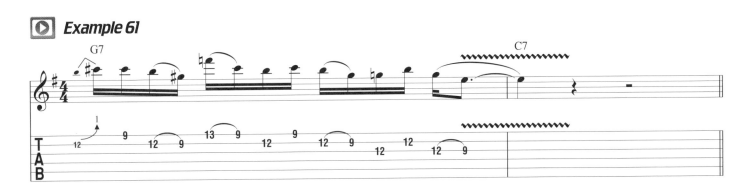

Much like Example 49, this ZZP #3 line in A♭ has a Lydian dominant feel with its use of the #4th tension within an A♭ triad in the first two beats, and the inclusion of the ♭7th on the upbeat of beat 3. How is that possible? Look at it this way: squeeze together the altered 9ths into a singular 2nd degree, and symmetrical diminished becomes a Lydian dominant scale. After a momentary rest, the 3rd of D♭ (F) is anticipated on the upbeat of beat 4.

Example 62

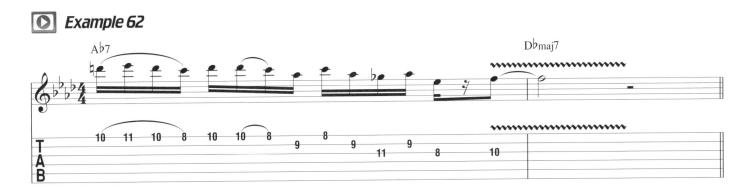

The final permutation on this catchy Vertical Positional lick idea is set in A within a VP #2 fingering. First, the bend is allowed to sing a bit longer since it rings out a cool-sounding #9 (C) over the A7. At the fourth 16th of beat 3, it strays from the original idea as it continues to descend with a repeating minor 3rd pull-off (F# to D#), eventually migrating to the target 3rd of D7 (F#) with a cool-sounding major 3rd dip from the ♭9.

Example 63

For the final major-3rd resolving symmetrical diminished line, 6ths are put to good use in this ZZP #2 line in B♭ going to E♭maj7. Notice the 6ths, though all ascending, are played in a disjunctive manner, lending an unusual flavor to the line. That playful awkwardness is subsided with a whole-step bend to the root (B♭) that eventually releases to a pull-off a half step below to the 3rd of E♭ (G).

Example 64

Resolving to Tonic Chord 5th

This group of four lines uses symmetrical diminished to resolve to the target tonic chord's perfect 5th. You'll notice that this chord tone is actually the root of the dominant chord—i.e., the root of the symmetrical diminished scale being used to create the tension. Though this book has hipped you to many lines under various conceptual umbrellas that end on the root, you can never be exposed to too many ideas. Every line you can get your ears and hands on should be considered buried treasure. One gem of note in this collection is what I call *ricochet phrasing*. Watch for it!

Nested minor 3rd intervals are used to great effect in this VP #1 B symmetrical diminished line at the upbeat of beat 2. After the initial back-and-forth between 6 and #4, you have descending minor 3rds spread out across the third and fourth beats. At one point, three quarters of a B°7 arpeggio are played before a descending major 3rd move is used to make way to B: the target 5th of the resolving chord.

Example 65

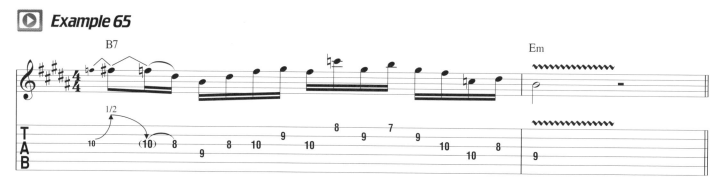

Revisiting the concept of permutations, this C symmetrical diminished line out of a ZZP #1 fingering takes on a more rhythmic permutation approach by condensing most of Example 17 from a two-bar line to a one-bar line. This was done by doubling up the eighth-note passages to 16th notes before chromatically walking up to the resolving 5th (C) of the next chord.

Example 66

Permuting another lick from earlier in the book, this C♯ symmetrical diminished line in VP #4 takes the ascending Scalene Right dominant diminished arpeggio run from the first half of Example 47 and breaks up the sequence. Beat 4 is adjusted to make a smooth transition to the anticipated half-step bend to the resolving chord's 5th (C♯).

▶ Example 67

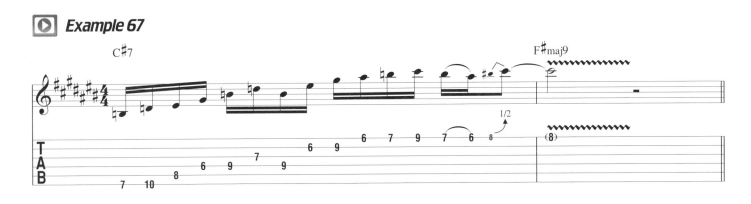

The D symmetrical diminished fingering in this line is a ZZP #4, but notice how the first note (the root note D) is played on the fifth fret, fifth string. This is reminiscent of the first symmetrical diminished fingering you learned back in Chapter 1—the Zig-Zag/Vertical Hybrid Positional—where you have a four-note-per-string instance snuck in there. While this book does not go down the four-note-per-string rabbit hole, that's not to say there's no value in the idea. As seen here, it makes an otherwise very difficult passage playable. What follows the first three 16th notes is another go-to in my symmetrical diminished trick bag. The idea is what I call *ricochet phrasing*. It starts on the fourth 16th of beat 1 with a sequence that progresses to the next note in the scale on the higher adjacent string—in this case, the sixth-fret G♯ (#4) on the fourth string—but immediately ricochets back to the fifth string for a hammer-on from F to F♯ (#9 to 3). I follow that with the same approach—albeit different fingering—for the next adjacent string pair in the scale before crossing the finish line for the resolution.

▶ Example 68

Resolving to Tonic Chord 7th

The final eight lines resolve to a tonic chord 7th of both types. The first four will resolve to a major 7th, and the final four will resolve to a dominant chord's ♭7th (remember, symmetrical diminished doesn't do well with minor chord resolutions). All the line construction components you've worked through thus far will be in play, as well as a concentrated focus on bending. All too often we guitar players sometimes forget to include our most valuable phrasing asset in the mix when learning about and/or developing new improvisational concepts. Bending is what makes guitar players sound vibey, organic, and real. Listeners and fellow musicians alike connect to a heartfelt bend at every turn. I've campaigned throughout this book to make the time you spend in developing your symmetrical diminished playing both musical and immediately applicable. For me, bending makes everything all that and more. Throughout these eight lines will be several bending approaches. The unique layouts in both symmetrical diminished Fingering Groups that set up all these new-fangled tactics you've explored also provide opportunity for some very cool, fresh takes on staple bending techniques. It's a win-win!

Kicking off these eight lines is an E♭ symmetrical diminished line in VP #1. It all starts with a singing whole-step bend to a biting #9 (F♯). The line continues to descend down the scale, which includes a half-step pre-bend to ♭7 (D♭) at the downbeat of beat 3. After a pull-off to the 5th (B♭), you'll play a 3rd (G) on the third 16th of beat 3 for the first of three times. The next will be on the upbeat of 4, serving as an anticipation to the implied A♭maj7, flowing into a back-and-forth instance that lands you on that same G via a whole-step bend at the fourth 16th of beat 1, bar 2. In both the second and third time G is played, it's the target major 7th resolution. In all three instances, it's played on various parts of the beat as well as with different phrasing. What you have here is another setting where a tone in the symmetrical diminished scale is common with a target chord tone of the resolving chord. To add color, it's shifted rhythmically.

▶ **Example 69**

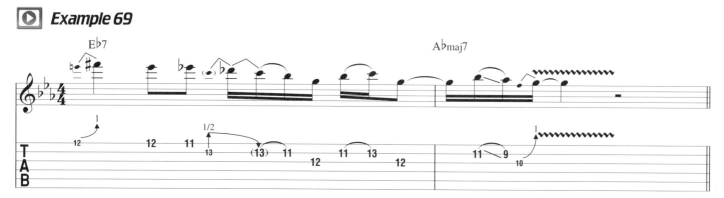

This ZZP #1 fingering in E symmetrical diminished launches with swiftly phrased ascending nested tritones on beat 1. The rhythmic tension subsides with a unison bend that's held until a pull-off to #9 (G) at the third triplet of beat 3. That same #9 is not only part of a direct diminished arpeggio, but more importantly, it's one half of the type of tight half-step melodic voice leading you want to go for. That G becomes a G♯ at the fourth 16th of beat 4, serving as a major 7th anticipation to the Amaj7. The icing on the cake is the stacking of 3rds in tandem above the resolving note, creating a Lydian sound over the resolving Amaj7 with a superimposed B major arpeggio.

▶ **Example 70**

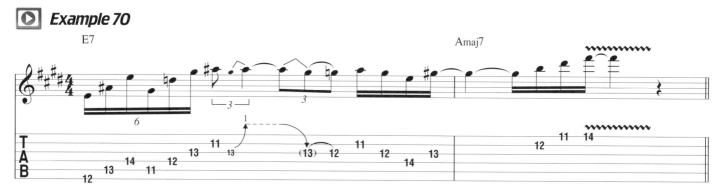

This symmetrical diminished idea in F using a VP #4 serves up not one, but two slightly different types of unison bends. Let's look at the one that commences the line. Here we have a half-step bend at the 12th fret, third string to the #9th (G♯). This is followed by an A note (3rd)—a half step higher—on the second string at the 10th fret. From there, the line travels up the scale to the C (5th) on the 13th fret. It is that same C that the following 12th-fret B is bent to. I call these single-string unison bends. While a unison bend such as the one in Example 69 is usually a bend that involves two strings—one lower adjacent string bending up to the pitch of the higher string to match it—the profit of a unison bend is clever phrasing of a common pitch between two strings. This is another, often overlooked way to phrase, and it should be a technique kept close and worked into your own phrasing. That same half-step bend releases to a pull-off to that same 10th-fret A, which ping pongs a ♭9 (G♭) before morphing into a major 7th anticipation of B♭maj7. That note's final role is to hang until the Satriani-esque descending pull-offs.

▶ **Example 71**

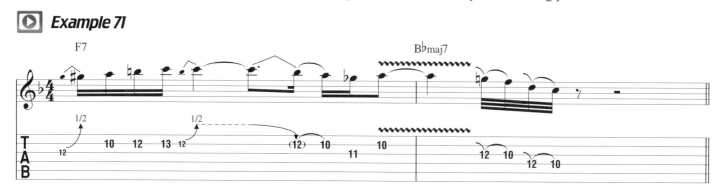

Nested major 6ths open this ZZP #4 F# symmetrical diminished line and proceed to a single-string unison bend of #4/♭5 (B#/C) on the second string at the downbeat of beat 2. The ascending pitch motion continues to C#, which kicks off a trio of backward-motion nested minor 3rds. The catch is that the third sequence (D#–F#) is phrased with a variation to add flavor. It starts with a whole-step bend with no release to the higher note (F#) from a 12th-fret E. The E is then played followed by the lower note of the sequence (D#) at the downbeat of beat 4. The line concludes with the ♭9 moving up a minor 3rd to set up the major 7th resolution on Bmaj7 (A#). Regarding minor 3rds used in this manner: they are one of my go-to intervals to bridge into resolving notes.

▶ **Example 72**

Here are the final four symmetrical diminished lines. They will resolve to a ♭7th while continuing to push your symmetrical diminished chops!

Rolling out the final four is a double diminished idea in triplets, with a descending Scalene Right dominant diminished arpeggio. I like to compare this type of dual diminished line to riding the Buccaneer at Six Flags. The first half of the line swings in one direction as described, climaxing with a half-step bend at the final triplet on beat 2, and then swings back up the VP #3 fingering with a Scalene Left direct diminished arpeggio, making a bee-line for the ♭7th of C7 (B♭) by way of anticipation.

▶ **Example 73**

Taking a more scalar approach, this ZZP #3-based line in A♭ throws out another same-string unison bend at the fourth 16th of beat 1. In this case, the 5th (E♭) is played first as a fretted note on the first string, 11th fret followed by a half-step bend from a half step below. As mentioned previously, you should keep this phrasing tool close. I encourage you to use it at will. In this case, it helps loosen up scalar passages so as not to sound too notey or stiff. In the second half of this symmetrical diminished run is an instance where another half-step bend going to the ♭7 (G♭) is played on the second 16th of beat 3, and then reiterated as a fretted note at the upbeat of beat 4, before handing off the ♭7 (C♭) to the D♭7 chord. Think of this as another way to make bends and their fretted-note clones interact to infuse your line with various phrasings of the same pitch. These are effective tools to help make a seemingly cerebral-sounding scale, such as symmetrical diminished, sound more organic and inviting.

▶ **Example 74**

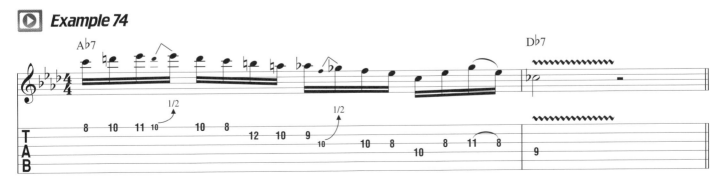

Foregoing a focus on bends just for a moment and staying scalar, the A symmetrical diminished line in VP #2 employs a sequence that hearkens back to the pattern-laden approaches presented in the beginning of the book. Taking advantage of the neatly packaged three-note-per-string layout of Vertical Positional, what you have is a four-note sequence that's made up of an ascending three-note-per-string sequence followed by the highest note of the lower adjacent string sequence. This covers the first two beats before the second half of the line runs up the scale in my self-patented ricochet phrasing, dressed in rapid 16th-note triplets. Given the swinging of directions, this is yet another ride on the Buccaneer that climaxes with a whole-step bend to the D7 target chord's ♭7 (C).

▶ Example 75

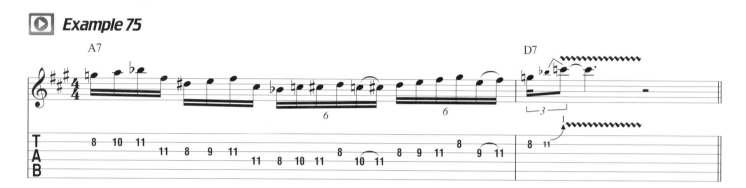

For the final outside guitar line with symmetrical diminished, I give you a bending trifecta that slips and slides through B♭ symmetrical diminished in a ZZP #2 configuration. There are three different bending scenarios starting with a second-string bend-and-release on beat 1 that rings out a ♭9 before dipping down the three-note-per-string sequence via a pull-off and a half-step slide. Next up is a whole-step bend to the root at the second triplet of beat 2 that starts an ascent up the scale on the first string, leading to the third and most important bend. This half-step bend rises to the 3rd (D) over the implied B♭7 chord, which, after release, is pulled off to the ♭9 and followed by a hammer to the resolving chord's ♭7 (D♭). This is classic, tight, half-step melodic voice leading—D to D♭. All this action is simmered with a soulful descending E♭ major arpeggio connecting to a chromatic walk down to the ♭7 of E♭.

▶ Example 76

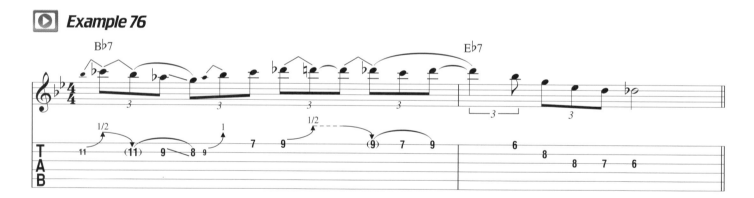

The next chapter is going to provide yet another way to organize this symmetrical system—this time through something called *harmonic connections*. It's a powerful tool I use every day to navigate my way through this cache of similar fingerings.

CHAPTER 5
HARMONIC CONNECTIONS

Having a strong awareness of scale degree layout is important and useful in your quest to play great outside lines with symmetrical diminished—even more so given the symmetrical nature of the scale and its resultant repetitious elements and offspring. What if there were a way to bolster your scale degree recognition skills as well as enhance your neck vision and command of symmetrical diminished? There is, and the way to do it is with *harmonic connections*, or more simply, chords. Much like the kid in *The Sixth Sense* saw dead people, I see chords—that is, chords that I'm only aware of. While playing symmetrical diminished lines, I visualize chords to help me better navigate the "chord-to-scale" tones in a given position. The better my vision is on this tip, the more effective my lines are playing over changes.

This chord-to-scale vision also helps me make a stronger connection to what I'm playing by helping give the scale a badge or mental avatar that I can use to visually label these symmetrically identical fingerings. This chapter will show you how you can, too.

TETRAD FOUNDATIONS

The foundation of the harmonic connections I see within the guitar's symmetrical diminished scale matrix is rooted in the drop 3 dominant seventh voicings played on the 6–4–3–2 string set:

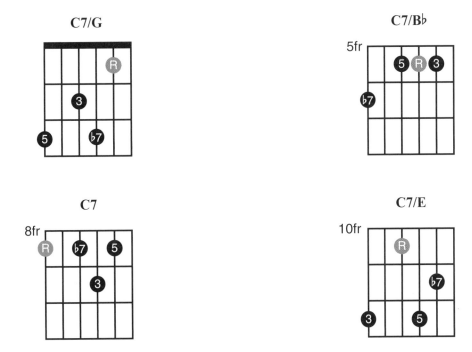

If you're not already familiar with them, get them under your fingers and be sure you're up to par with their voicing layout. A few things to keep in mind about what you see here before going forward:

- Make sure you have instant recall, if not unconscious knowledge, of the chord tones in each chord. From the chord tones are the connections to the rest of the scale degrees.

- Since these drop 3 voicings don't share common tones for you to establish a connective vision, you'll need to establish an alternative that's quick and void of exceptions. One way is to see the whole-step connection from every chord's ♭7th to the next chord's root, or vice versa, as you go up and down the neck.

With these chords firmly established both under your fingers and in your mind, they can serve you in two ways as foundations for symmetrical diminished visualizations. We'll start with diminished seventh chord connections.

Diminished Seventh Chord Connection

The 6–4–3–2 dominant seventh chords can be made into a series of four symmetrically related, identical diminished seventh chords by lowering the 3rd, 5th, and 7th of each chord by a half step. They look like this:

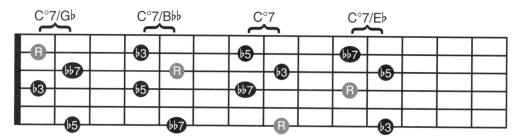

In regards to the now-established symmetrical diminished elements, including scale degrees and the two types of nested diminished seventh arpeggios concepts, let's look at a set of diminished seventh chords from a G root.

Talking the Symmetrical Diminished Talk

As you investigate the following diminished seventh chords, you'll come across some unorthodox, yet intentional and necessary uses of enharmonics in the chord names—specifically with slash bass notes. This is done in the name of staying consistent with the symmetrical diminished concepts you're studying in this book. When all this new information has settled in, you'll be able to freely interchange musical theory correctness and everyday interval slang.

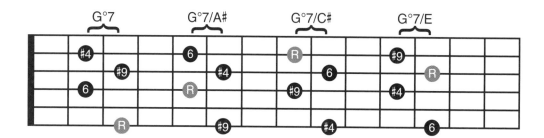

These four chords are your direct diminished connections (introduced in Chapter 3). The way they connect to the Zig-Zag Positional Group seen in Chapter 2 is by each chord's lowest note (sixth string), which is the starting note of each of the four scales shown in the charts on page 15.

Symmetrical Diminished 101 Reminder

Back in Chapter 1, the ground work was laid for a solid understanding of basic symmetrical diminished knowledge. Part of that knowledge was the awareness of the scale degrees and their upper extension counterparts:

$$♭2/♯2 = ♭9/♯9$$
$$♯4/♭5 = ♯11$$
$$6 = 13$$

Additionally, there was attention paid to the inherent enharmonics. Throughout this chapter, you'll see scale degrees in the form of chord tones making jumps to extensions, as well as being named seemingly strange enharmonic denominations. Keep in mind it's all for the purposes of understanding a concept that's wrought with confusion and complex repeating, as well as overlapping properties.

Extended Dominant Chord Foundation

The second of the two symmetrical diminished visualization approaches connects with the dominant diminished concept and the Vertical Positional Group. Once again, the chords utilized are drop 3 dominant seventh chords on the 6–4–3–2 strings, but this time the focus is on the root-position and second-inversion dominant seventh chords only. However, keep in mind that the first- and third-inversion chords serve as a way to bridge the two chords you'll be focusing on. While it requires a few more steps, it's the one I use most often.

Shifting back to a C root, the map below shows how a pair of root-position and second-inversion drop 3 C7 chords serves as the foundation for a system of extensions and alterations that culminate into what I refer to as *Tritone Mirror Chords*. Check it out:

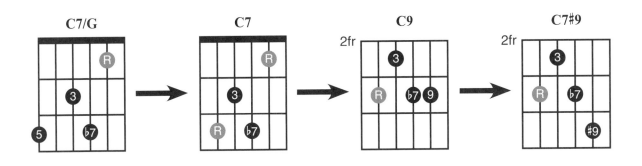

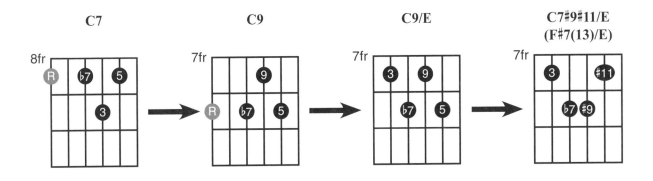

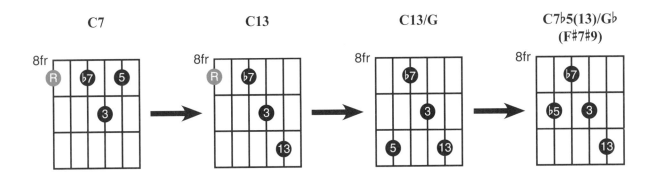

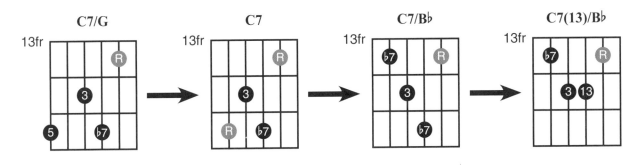

In the first and fourth rows where we see C7/G, the first phase of change is shifting over the 5th (G) in the bass to the next adjacent string, making that note the root. The middle rows go their separate ways with the second row C7 dropping its 3rd down a whole step to create a C9 with no 3rd, while the third row C7 raises its 5th a whole step, adding an upper extension in the form of a 13th. In regards to the former, technically speaking, that chord is a C7sus2, but for our purposes, the liberty afforded by common guitar harmony shortcuts serves up an acceptable C9 naming. The next phase for the first row is moving its higher octave root up a whole step to create a go-to middle-four-string dominant ninth. The bottom row goes through a two-step process, becoming a C13/B♭, as the root goes down a whole step to the ♭7, and the ♭7 goes down a half step to become a 13th. Looking at this from the perspective of the third column, all four rows are where you'll see each chord become a bona fide extended dominant chord in the form of a dominant ninth or dominant 13th. Take note of each bass note as each chord tone of a basic dominant seventh is represented. The fourth column is what I'm building up to. It's where you'll see the intended tritone mirror chord symmetrical diminished visualization system unfold.

Tritone Mirror Chords

The tritone mirror chords visualization is a symmetrical concept, but with one caveat. The catch is there are two pairs of symmetrical chords. The interval between each pair is a tritone (three whole steps) as seen here:

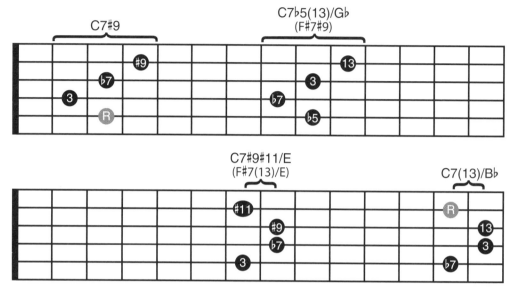

Also like the diminished seventh chords, they will serve as visual reference points helping you navigate your way through a sea of identical scale fingerings.

Chord-to-Scale Exercises

To begin to see your own chord avatars, you need to put the time in applying these harmonic connections. The following exercises are just some examples (see note below) of what you can use to help establish and maintain a solid symmetrical diminished chord-to-scale vision. You'll find exercises for diminished seventh chord connections as well as tritone mirror chords. Notice how each exercise starts and ends on a reference point (mostly chords), much like a spelling bee. This is to help drive home the visual connection between the chord and the scales local to it.

> **Always Make It Count**
> When it comes to exercises, I keep two things in mind:
>
> - Make the exercises applicable
> - Avoid playing an exercise as-is for long periods
>
> All exercises I design for myself are tailor-made to enhance the aspects of my playing I want to build on. You'll notice in these exercises there's liberal use of legato and, in many cases, it occurs on the off-beat 16ths (second and fourth 16th). This is a big part of my phrasing, and it took a lot of work to make it sound natural. It only came to be after cutting right to the chase and committing to it. Too many times, I see intermediate to early advanced players investing precious practice time into exercises that contain one or more elements that are not directly related to their goals. Furthermore—and this brings me to my second requirement—they play the same exercises ad nauseam, never even considering variations. If your intentions are rooted in high-level improvisation with a focus on developing your own voice (that's a safe bet if you're reading this book and you've made it this far), your approach should be the contrary. You should learn an exercise, make any changes necessary to fit your playing goals, get some mileage out of it, and then periodically shuffle the deck, so to speak. The "shuffling" can be ever-so-slight, such as a few notes shifted or a rhythmic element changed, or something more involved, such as learning the exercises backwards. Whatever you do, be sure to always make your practice count by making it work for you, as opposed to working for the exercise.

This first trio of exercises focuses on a direct diminished seventh vision making use of the Zig-Zag Positional fingerings laid out for you in Chapter 2, where these scales were first introduced. Each of the three exercises starts off with the same motif within the Zig-Zag Positional #1 fingering on the following adjacent string sets: E–B, D–G, and E–A. It's an ascending/descending run on the signature half step/whole step, whole step/half step adjacent string pattern, peppered with phrasing-specific legato. The idea is to show how each of the four scales offers up the same motif with nearly the same phrasing, while getting familiar with the necessary adjustments. How each of the motives plays out is what stamps the identity to each of the symmetrical fingerings that should be connected to the chord. Speaking of this, notice that the chords are played at the beginning and ending of the line idea—much like a middle schooler in a spelling bee. That's meant to drive home the harmonic connection: that chord-to-scale vision!

Feel free to start with a straight alternate picking approach if the legato instances prove to be too tricky at first.

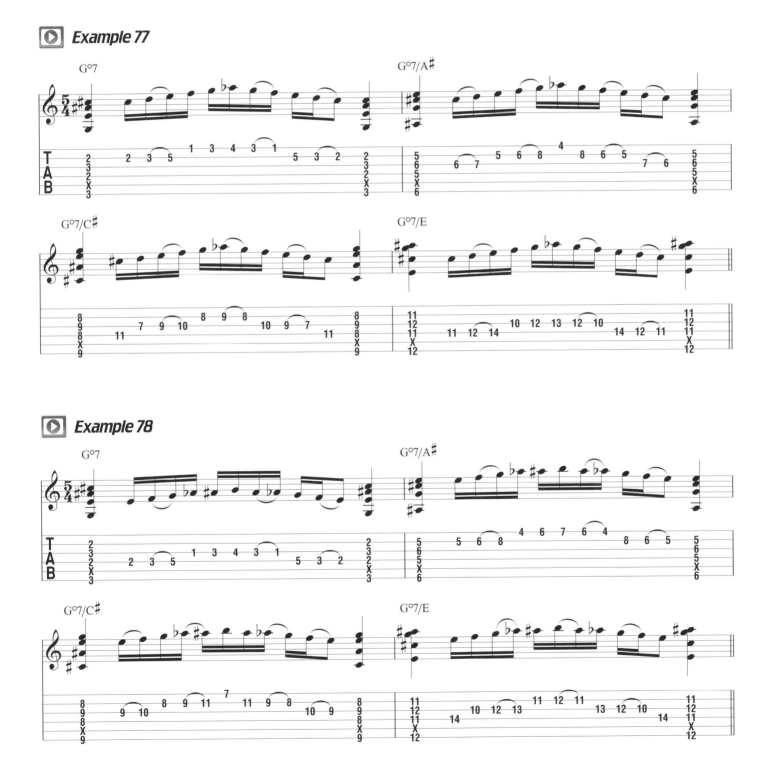

Example 79

The next set of exercises focuses on the dominant diminished vision connection to tritone mirror chords by way of the Vertical Positional Group in C. While the approach is changed, the goal remains the same: make harmonic connections, allowing symmetrical fingerings to become unique and powerful melodic devices.

Instead of hammering the chords by way of the spelling bee approach with the chords being played at the beginning and end of each line, the following exercises only see the chord played on the downbeat. Another change is the way the chord-to-scale relationship is being established. This time, the chords are followed by longer lines that end with the lowest root note of each of the four fingerings played on the upbeat. Those position-specific locations of the root are what connect each of the fingerings to each of the chords.

Example 80

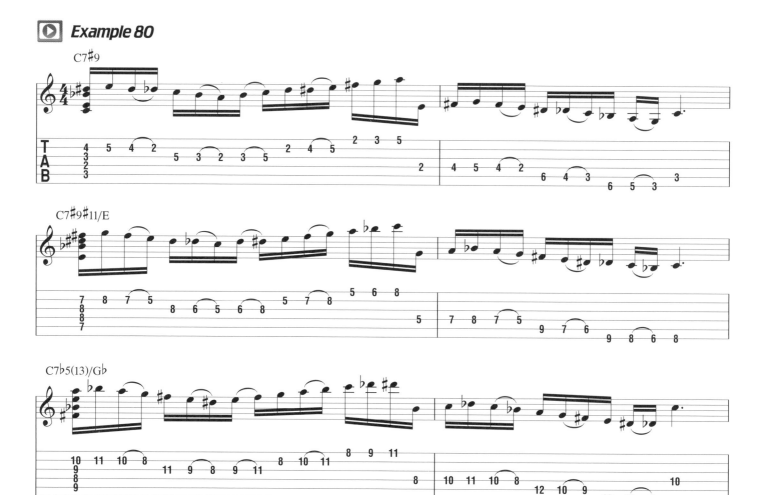

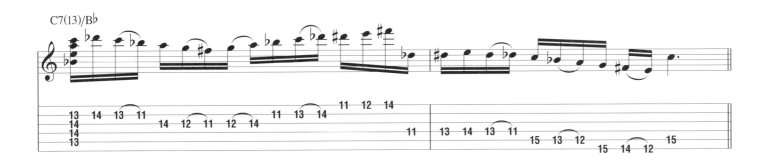

C7(13)/Bb

This second set of dominant diminished-based exercises takes the same approach to the Vertical Positional fingerings by ending lines on position-specific roots. This time, the lines make use of the nested major 6ths played in an alternate motion, as first learned in Chapter 3.

▶ Example 81

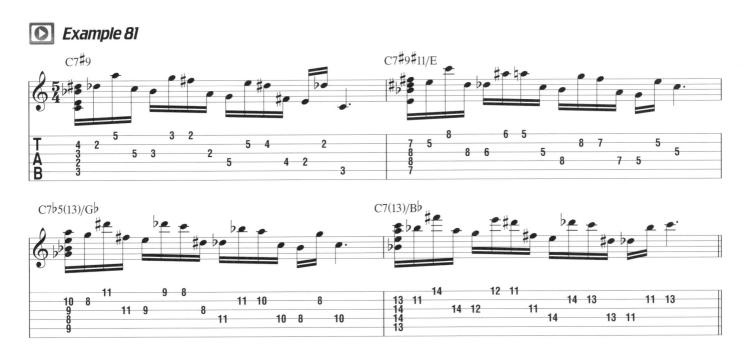

Once again, these are just some ideas to establish and maintain a solid harmonic connection to the direct and dominant diminished chord-to-scale visions. The more you come up with, the stronger the connection will be. In the upcoming final chapter, you'll learn a fresh, new way to approach constructing lines with the symmetrical diminished scale.

CHAPTER 6

SYMMETRICAL DIMINISHED PENTATONIC SCALES

The quest for great-sounding lines is an ongoing one for all players at every level. That quest can and should lead you down all sorts of paths—even ones you pave for yourself. I have a final concept for you to explore that's just that type of path: symmetrical diminished pentatonic scales. The fact is pentatonic scales are not just regulated to minor and major (or even their other three modal starting points). The concept behind pentatonic is just that: a concept. It's one that can be applied and reapplied at will, and that's precisely what I did with this group of five scales. Before you start scratching your head or racing to your computer to do a search, stop. You're not going to find these anywhere else. This is one of many uncharted paths that I set myself on, trawling for new ideas that I may have otherwise never come across.

So, why pentatonic scales at any rate, you ask? For starters, I'm a big fan of two-note-per-string sequences for phrasing, especially with a heavy lean towards legato and bending. What's more, I like the challenge of taking a playing tool that's very ingrained in my head and hands and morphing it into something altogether different, yet the same.

In this chapter, you'll learn about the reasoning and procedure behind the creation of four sets of pentatonic scale formulas all built from an A root. You'll find five scales per set—one that starts and ends on each degree—as well as a two-bar line for each and every scale to wail on. That's 20 in all! It's up to you to use your symmetrical diminished neck vision to map out fingerings. You're also equipped with ample symmetrical diminished theoretical chops to assess the scale degree layouts. This party is licks only!

I sincerely hope this idea, and the method in which it was brought to life, inspires you to pave your own unique paths to inspiring-sounding symmetrical diminished lines!

One More Decoded Disclaimer

Keeping consistent with this book's avant-garde naming convention and abbreviations, each of the four sets of five pentatonic scales will follow a unique naming format. The first and last parts will be common. The first part addresses their five-note makeup with the title Symmetrical Diminished Pentatonic, shortened to SDP. Unlike the convention set by the VP and ZZP Groups, where numbers 1–4 appended each scale, the last part of these names will instead use the names of the first five letters of the Greek alphabet: Alpha, Beta, Gamma, Delta, and Epsilon. In between these two elements is the actual scalar formula.

Let's look at an example. The first formula you'll check out is 1–#9–#4–5–♭7. The designations will be as follows:

- SDP 1–#9–#4–5–♭7 Alpha: Starts on the root
- SDP 1–#9–#4–5–♭7 Beta: Starts on #9
- SDP 1–#9–#4–5–♭7 Gamma: Starts on #4
- SDP 1–#9–#4–5–♭7 Delta: Starts on 5
- SDP 1–#9–#4–5–♭7 Epsilon: Starts on ♭7

In regards to the scale degree usage, it adheres to the symmetrical diminished degree verbiage and keeps consistent with the overall approach and teachings of this book.

SDP 1–#9–#4–5–♭7

The custom pentatonic scale sets you're about to investigate are five-note scales whose formulae are derived from a larger formula-base—in this case symmetrical diminished. The first set is based off a conventional minor pentatonic construction: 1–♭3–4–5–♭7. From symmetrical diminished, I chose the scale degrees that most closely resemble that formula while still containing symmetrical diminished tensions. What I came up with is this:

1–#9–#4–5–♭7

Roadmap

This formula suitably sets up a phrasing architecture I'm very familiar with. Here's what they look like:

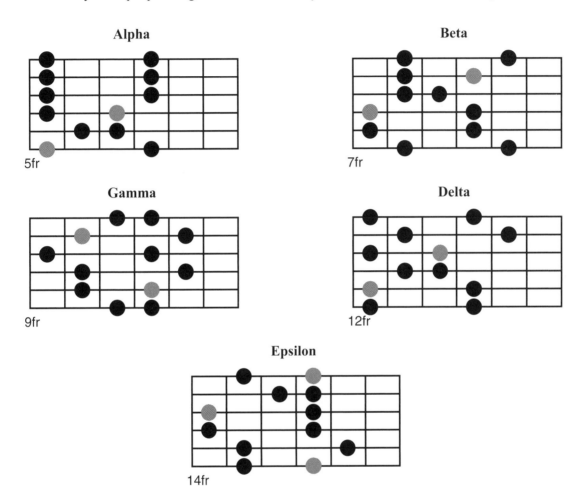

Lines

With these scales, I can freely improvise fiery minor blues-sounding lines that come off as unexpected rock licks. They sound deliciously out when played over dominant seventh and qualifying altered dominant seventh chords. Here are five to take for a ride. Keep in mind that the goal for this set was to provide a melodic vehicle to play symmetrical diminished flavors within a relative environment. If you're a rocker at heart, you'll feel right at home with this quintet!

▶ Example 82

SDP 1–#9–#4-5-♭7 Alpha

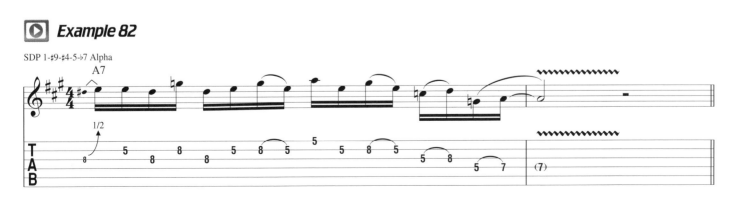

Example 83

SDP 1-#9-#4-5-♭7 Beta

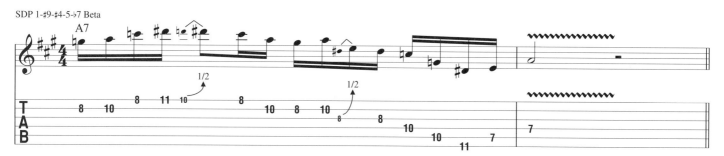

Example 84

SDP 1-#9-#4-5-♭7 Gamma

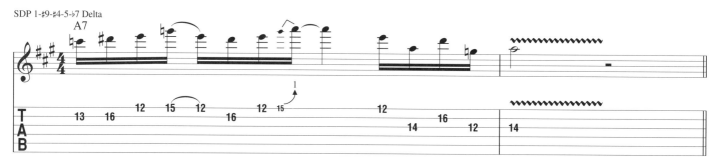

Example 85

SDP 1-#9-#4-5-♭7 Delta

Example 86

SDP 1-#9-#4-5-♭7 Epsilon

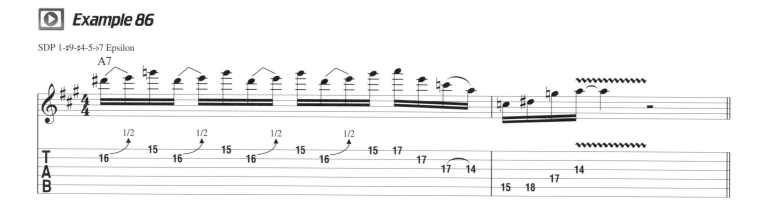

SDP 1–#9–3–#4–6

The next set veers from a minor pentatonic/minor blues approach. Instead it takes a major pentatonic scale formula, 1–2–3–5–6, and twists it through a symmetrical diminished metamorphosis. Once again, I chose the symmetrical scale degrees that most closely resemble that formula while still containing symmetrical diminished tensions. What I came up with is this:

1–#9–3–#4–6

Roadmap

The roadmap is quite different but still maintains the two-note-per-string setup I'm after. Dig into these and be sure to do your own scale degree layout. You're going to need it!

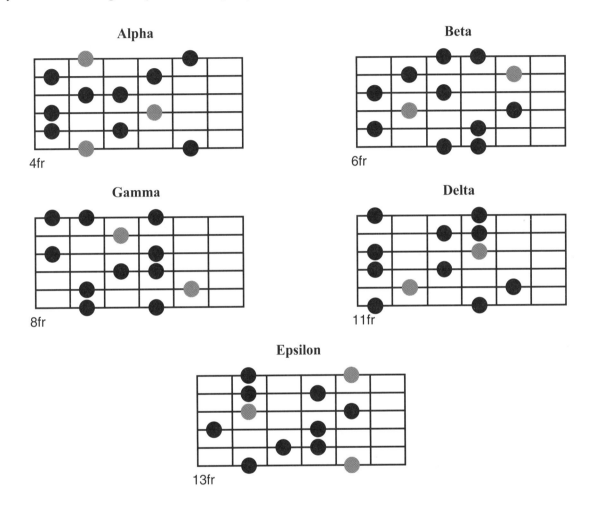

Lines

This scale formula is much different than the first custom symmetrical diminished pentatonic formula and therefore creates very different-sounding lines. That said, watch for similar phrasing elements just the same. Rock these five and stay conscious of the scale degrees. In the next two sections, I'm going to use these lines as the foundation for stationary permutations.

Feral Bend Alert

In Example 88 you'll notice a slow, stiff upper lip-inducing half-step bend in bar 1 on the upbeat of beat 2. It's a slick phrasing tool where an ascending grace-note slide starting from the 6th degree (F#) travels up a mere whole step on a 1-1/2 step journey to the root. The final leg of the ascension is completed by way of a half-step bend from a non-diatonic major 7th degree. Do not get caught up by this seemingly alien intruder note: G#. This is not the first time tones outside the symmetrical diminished scale have been introduced in these licks and should not be your last going forward. In addition to being open to strategically adding notes outside the symmetrical diminished scale to your licks, take note of the feral power of half-step below approach bends and watch for this one again in Examples 93 and 98.

Example 87

SDP 1-♯9-3-♯4-6 Alpha

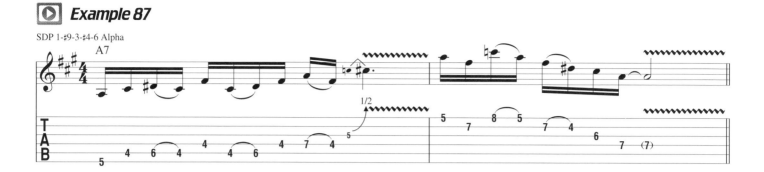

Example 88

SDP 1-♯9-3-♯4-6 Beta

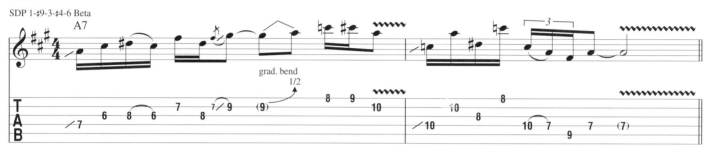

Example 89

SDP 1-♯9-3-♯4-6 Gamma

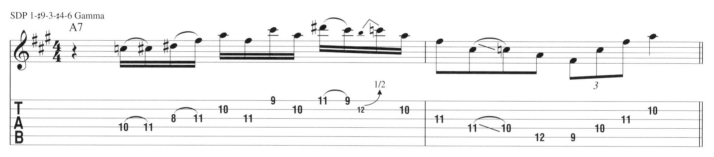

Example 90

SDP 1-♯9-3-♯4-6 Delta

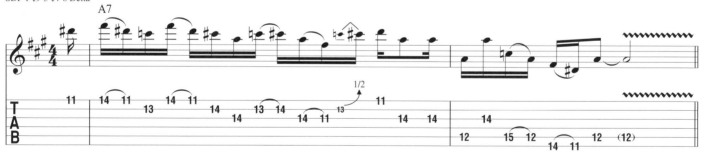

Example 91

SDP 1-♯9-3-♯4-6 Epsilon

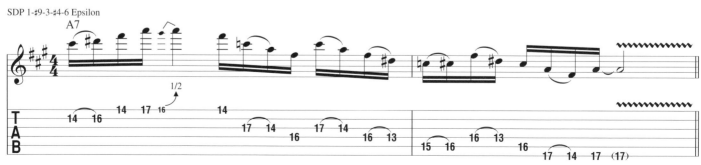

SDP 1–♭9–3–♯4–6

Continuing the symmetrical diminished metamorphosis, this transformation simply pulls a switcheroo in the altered 9's category, giving this scale formula a ♭9. While this is but one note's difference, the effect is undeniable and sounds very cool—not to mention it's just fun to play. This is what it looks like:

1–♭9–3–♯4–6

Roadmap
Here's the roadmap for this ♭9-propelled custom symmetrical diminished pentatonic.

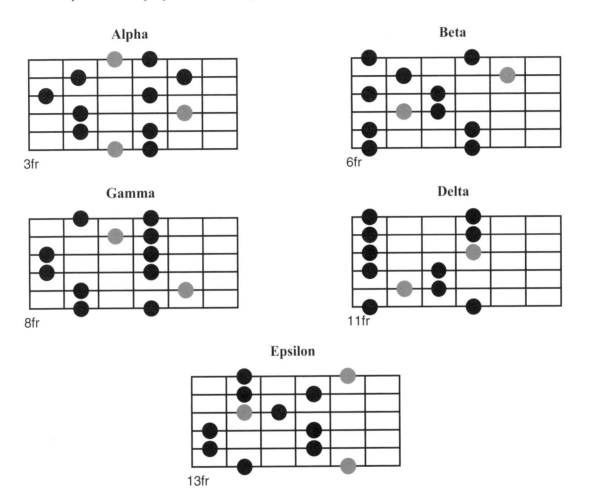

Lines
As mentioned earlier, the following five lines are the results of a stationary permutation. The scales from which the changes were applied are the previous five lines born of the SDP 1–♯9–3–♯4–6 set. This is a process I often engage in and benefit from highly. On the surface level, it presents myriad playing challenges that remind me to never underestimate how much one note can throw a line in a completely different direction. That said, you'll notice the permutations are not always literal to the very last note. Some necessary as well as beneficial changes are made to accommodate the changes (and ultimately keep me musical). The ultimate goal is to be able to do this freely in real time. To do that, substantial time is dedicated to this process. Enjoy your first foray.

Example 92

SDP 1-♭9-3-♯4-6 Alpha

Example 93

SDP 1-♭9-3-♯4-6 Beta

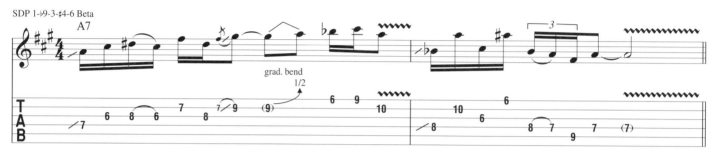

Example 94

SDP 1-♭9-3-♯4-6 Gamma

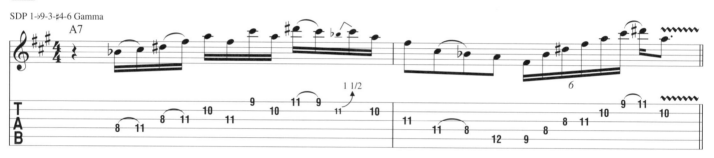

Example 95

SDP 1-♭9-3-♯4-6 Delta

Example 96

SDP 1-♭9-3-♯4-6 Epsilon

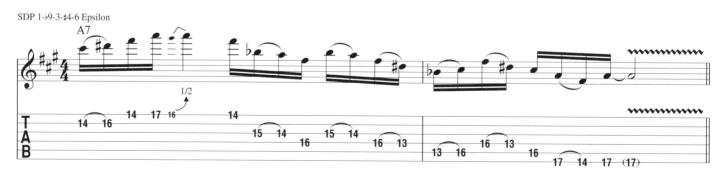

SDP 1–♭9–3–♯4–♭7

This last set is another symmetrical diminished pentatonic conversion, this time pushing the 6th degree up to a ♭7th, thus providing the crucial dominant seventh tritone between the 3 and ♭7 for the first time. Again, you can hear just how effective changing one note can be. In some cases, it changes even more so on the playing front. With the mutation, the formula reads like this:

$$1–♭9–3–♯4–♭7$$

Roadmap

The roadmap looks like this:

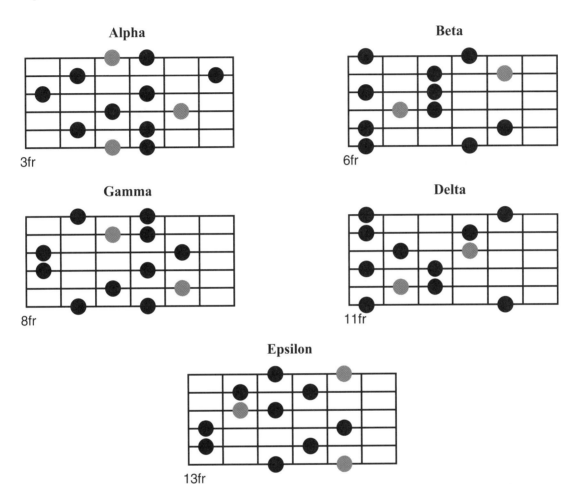

Lines

Finally, the mutated lines sound like this!

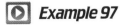 **Example 97**

SDP 1-♭9-3-♯4-♭7 Alpha

▶ Example 98

SDP 1-♭9-3-#4-♭7 Beta

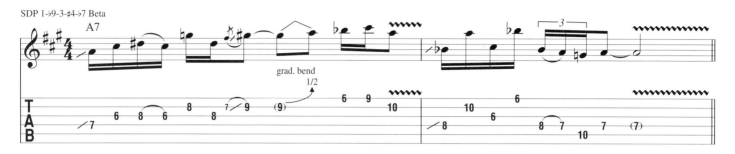

▶ Example 99

SDP 1-♭9-3-#4-♭7 Gamma

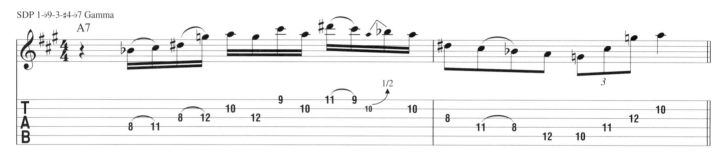

▶ Example 100

SDP 1-♭9-3-#4-♭7 Delta

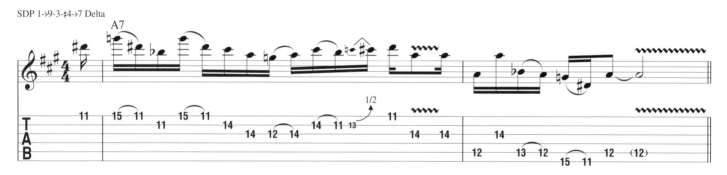

▶ Example 101

SDP 1-♭9-3-#4-♭7 Epsilon

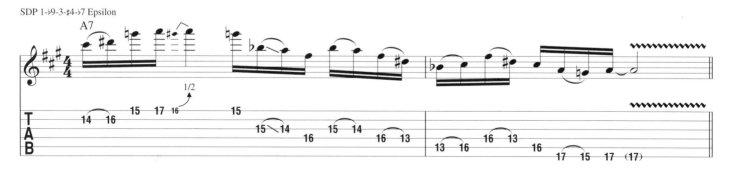